MEN-AT-ARMS SERIE

EDITOR: MARTIN WINDR

Ancient Armies of the Middle East

Text *by* TERENCE WISE

Colour plates *by* ANGUS McBRIDE

OSPREY PUBLISHING LONDON

Published in 1981 by
Osprey Publishing Ltd,
59 Grosvenor Street, London, W1X 9DA
© Copyright 1981 Osprey Publishing Ltd
Reprinted 1982, 1984, 1985, 1986, 1987, 1988, 1990

ISBN 0 85045 384 4

Filmset in Great Britain
Printed in Hong Kong

Sources

Baikie, J. *The Story of the Pharaohs*. London 1917.
Bible, Old Testament.
Botta, P. E. *The Buried City of the East: Nineveh*. London 1851.
Boudet, J. (ed) *The Ancient Art of Warfare. Vol 1*. London 1966.
Cleator, P. E. *Weapons of War*. London 1967.
Cottrell, L. *The Anvil of Civilization*. New York 1957.
Curtis, J. *Wheeled Vehicles in Ancient Western Asia*. London 1975.
Fairservis, W. A. *The Ancient Kingdoms of the Nile*. New York 1962.
Gonen, R. *Weapons of the Ancient World*. London 1975.
Gurney, O. R. *The Hittites*. Harmondsworth 1952.
Herodotus. *The Histories*. Harmondsworth 1954.
Herzog, C., & Gichon, M. *Battles of the Bible*. London 1978.
Hinz, W. (trans J. Barnes) *The Lost World of Elam*. London 1972.
Keller, W. (trans W. Neil) *The Bible as History*. London 1956.
Keller, W. (trans W. Neil) *The Bible as History in pictures*.
  London 1964.
Layard, A. H. *Nineveh and its Remains*. London 1867.
Magnusson, M. *The Archaeology of the Bible Lands*. London 1977.
Maspero, G. *Life in Ancient Egypt and Assyria*. London 1892.
Rawlinson, G. *History of Ancient Egypt. Vol 1*. London 1881.
Wilkinson, Sir J. G. *A Popular Account of the Ancient Egyptians.
  Vols 1 & 2*. London 1890.
Yadin, Y. (trans M. Pearlman) *The Art of Warfare in Biblical Lands*.
  London 1963.

Introduction

This title covers a vast span of the history of a large and important part of the world, so it is important to set out the limits of this book. Firstly, 'Middle East' is itself a modern and rather imprecise term: it is used here to describe Israel, Lebanon, Syria, Jordan, Iraq, Egypt, the northernmost parts of the Sudan and Saudi Arabia, and that region of western Asia which now forms the greater part of Turkey—the Asia Minor of ancient history.

Secondly, the period chosen coincides with that often referred to in military terms as the Age of the Chariot, but I have taken 3100 B.C. as my starting point, since that is approximately the date at which history began to be recorded in the Middle East, coinciding with the beginning of the Bronze Age in that area; and have ended with the obliteration of the Assyrian Empire in 612 B.C. Apart from a brief return to independence for Babylonia, the fall of Assyria marked the beginning of the domination of the Middle East by the Medes, Persians and Greeks—all peoples from outside our chosen area.

Thirdly, although the period and area encompass over a dozen civilizations, it is inevitable that the 'Great Powers' of their day should dominate this work: the reader will find here much more on Egypt and Assyria than on their lesser neighbours. This is as it should be, and is naturally determined to some extent by the information available: we know much of the Assyrians, but little of the Elamites, for example.

Finally, the scope of the book combined with the fluid state of the population of the Middle East in ancient times, has made it necessary to include a lengthy chronology and some detail of the peoples involved, so that it may be understood who the various peoples were and what were their rôles in history. The information on their armies, arms and armour is drawn partly from the early writings of these peoples, but mainly from wall paintings, reliefs, and other archaeological finds.

Information culled from such sources is liable to wide variations of interpretation, but there is no room here to pursue the pros and cons of such

The renowned Pharaoh Rameses II, who extended Egyptian rule over the Kush and part of Arabia, and fought the Hittites for 15 years. Compare with Plate C and commentary on p. 37. (Author's collection)

Model soldiers from the tomb of Mesehti at Assuit, Middle Kingdom (2133–1786). These are believed to represent Nubian mercenaries. Their bow is shown as the simple or 'self' bow, not the more advanced double-convex bow of the Egyptians. (Egyptian Museum, Cairo)

matters. I have corrected some of the most glaring errors, first made during the last century and perpetuated in popular works ever since, and have advanced some thoughts of my own, but would refer the reader in particular to the works of Professor Yadin, Dr Keller and Magnus Magnusson for up-to-date appraisals of archaeological discoveries.

There is a surprising gap in modern popular works on military history when it comes to the Middle East of ancient times. I hope this small 'primer' will arouse sufficient curiosity to encourage the reader to pursue further a subject which is surely worthy of more interest—the very birth of recorded military history in the 'cradle of civilization'.

Chronology

(All dates are approximate)

B.C. **3500** *Mesopotamia:* Semitic population of southern Mesopotamia invaded or infiltrated by non-Semitic race which founds a collection of city-states known collectively as Sumer.

3100 *Mesopotamia:* Pictographic writing commences. *Egypt:* Unification of Upper and Lower Egypt by Menes, founder of I Dynasty, centred on Memphis.

3000 Early Bronze Age: Believed introduced by Sumerians. *Mesopotamia:* Assyrians first appear in upland plains of north-eastern Mesopotamia.

2980 *Egypt:* Death of Menes. Egypt divided into two kingdoms by his sons.

2686 *Egypt:* Beginning of Old Kingdom (III–VI Dynasties).

2680 *Mesopotamia:* First mention of Elamites, defeated by Sumerians of Kish. Prior to this it would appear the Elamites may have had some supremacy over Mesopotamia.

2500 First literary texts. *Mesopotamia:* Sumerian cities first united under one king (I Dynasty of Ur).

2400 *Syria:* Rise of Canaanite empire based on Ebla.

2350 *Mesopotamia:* Subjugation of Sumer by Semitic people led by Sargon, who founds capital at Akkad. *Egypt:* Old Kingdom vanishes in wave of chaos created by civil wars and invasions from east.

2325 *Mesopotamia:* Elam and Mari

subjugated by Akkadians.

2285 *Mesopotamia:* Gutians, a mountain people from north-east, conquer Akkad and Elam.

2225 *Mesopotamia:* Oldest known inscription of an Assyrian prince, Zariku of Ashur.

2181–2133 *Egypt:* 1st Intermediate Period (VII–X Dynasties).

2133–1991 *Egypt:* Middle Kingdom (XI–XII Dynasties). In XI Dynasty the princes of Thebes gradually reunite Egypt to create the Middle Kingdom, centred on Thebes.

2100 *Mesopotamia:* Sumerians regain supremacy under III Dynasty of Ur.

2030 *Mesopotamia:* Elam re-emerges as

a federation of cities under one king.

2010 *Mesopotamia:* Northern Mesopotamia is overrun by fresh waves of Semites (Amorites) from the west.

2000 *Mesopotamia:* 1st (Old) Babylonian Empire established by Amorites with capital at Babylon. Hurrians (Biblical 'Horites') appear from Caucasus Mountains region and establish kingdom of Mitanni between upper Tigris and Euphrates. *Asia Minor:* Hittites emerge as major power in northern and central Asia Minor.

2000–1750 *Syria:* Emergence of Mari as chief city-state of middle Euphrates.

1991–1786 *Egypt:* Under XII Dynasty Egypt

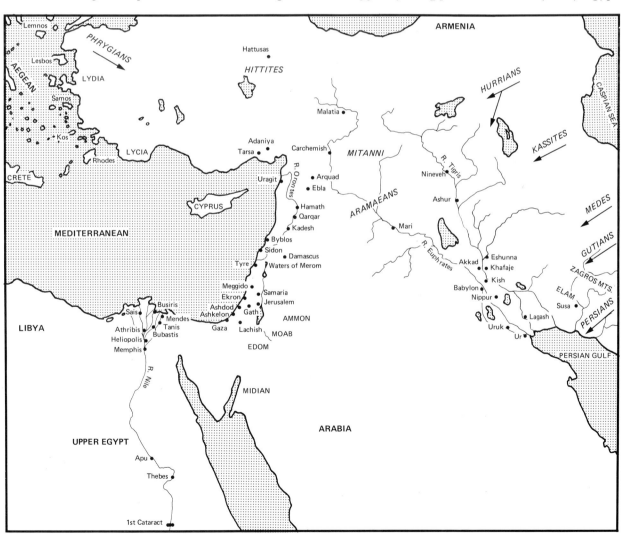

Elamite warriors taken from Assyrian reliefs. The chariot apparently consists of a flat bed without either front or sides, though the 'mudguards' may be a low, curved side rather like those of the British chariot. The war carts were of similar design but with between 12 and 16 spokes to the wheels, no 'mudguards', and a crew of three to four men. In the carts the men are all shown sitting, two being archers who faced front and rear or front only. The draught animals are often shown with ears resembling those of a mule. (From Layard & Maspero)

expands southwards into Nubia and lower Sudan, and eastwards towards Syria.

1900 *Mesopotamia:* Assyria expands to form the Old Empire based on Ashur.

1786–1567 *Egypt:* 2nd Intermediate Period (XIII–XVII Dynasties).

1764 *Mesopotamia:* Elamites conquered by Hammurabi of Babylon.

1750 *Syria:* Mari destroyed by Hammurabi.

1730 *Mesopotamia:* Kassites, a barbarian mountain people, begin to infiltrate from north-east.

1725 *Mesopotamia:* Babylon Empire under Hammurabi achieves dominance over all Mesopotamia.

Old Assyrian Empire is amongst those subjugated.

1700–1550 *Egypt:* Egypt is ruled by an Asiatic people, colloquially termed the Hyksòs.

1590 *Mesopotamia:* Hittites begin large scale expansion (Old Empire).

1576 *Egypt:* Hyksòs expelled, their Nubian allies reconquered, and Egypt reunited for a magnificent new era known as the New Kingdom, XVIII–XX Dynasties (1567–1320).

1550 *Mesopotamia:* Hittite pressure on Babylonian Empire from north-west enables Kassites to overrun southern Mesopotamia and establish a kingdom. Hittites begin to expand southwards into Syria.

1530 *Mesopotamia:* Kassites take over Babylonian Empire.

1500 *Mesopotamia:* For next 700 years there is infiltration into southern Mesopotamia by a Semitic desert people known as the Chaldeans, and it is they who provide much of the vitality shown by the Babylonian Empire at this time in its constant struggle against Assyrian domination.

1490 *Egypt:* Empire extended southwards beyond Fifth Cataract, westwards into Libya, and eastwards into Palestine.

1475 *Asia Minor:* Hittite Empire begins to threaten Egypt's expansion into Palestine and Syria.

1468 *Syria:* Hittite advance southwards halted by Egyptians at Megiddo.

1445 *Egypt:* Egyptians penetrate into Mesopotamia.

1380 *Mesopotamia:* Assyria begins rise to dominance.

1375 *Asia Minor:* Hittites expand again to overrun Babylonian Empire and once more enter Syria.

1355 *Syria:* Hittites conquer kingdom of Mitanni.

1350 *Syria:* Hittites establish control over Syria and threaten Egypt's position in Palestine.

1288 *Syria:* Egyptians halt Hittites at Kadesh and negotiate peace: Syria to the Hittites, Palestine to Egypt. *Mesopotamia:* Elamites seize opportunity of curtailment of Hittite power to regain their independence and subsequently enjoy a golden age.

1273 *Mesopotamia:* Hittites declare war on rapidly expanding Assyrian Empire. Thereafter the power of the Hittites declines rapidly due to wars with Assyria in the east, invasions by the Sea Peoples from the west, and internal disorders. When the empire finally disintegrates, *circa* 1220–1200, new independent kingdoms are founded at Malatia, Zinjirli, Carchemish, Tell Halaf and other places in northern Syria.

1230 *Asia Minor:* First assaults by Sea Peoples.

1226 *Mesopotamia:* Elam conquers Nippur in central Babylonia and forces Kassite king to flee. Thereafter Elam comes gradually under Assyrian dominance.

1225 *Syria:* Traditional date of Israel's conquest of Canaan.

1220 *Asia Minor:* Severe famine. Grain ships sent from Egypt.

1217 *Egypt:* Starving Libyans begin to cross border into Delta.

1206 *Mesopotamia:* Kassites lose Babylonia to expanding Assyrian Empire, with its capital at Nineveh.

1200 The Iron Age: The whole Middle East is in a turmoil as continued famine creates a vortex of migrations. Cyprus had been engulfed by the Sea Peoples, who then advanced on land through (and in ships along the coasts of) Asia Minor, Syria and Palestine, and are only halted at the borders of Egypt, *circa* 1190. Uragit and other coastal cities in Canaan are overwhelmed by these invasions; Rameses III, who defeats the Sea Peoples but does not crush them, wisely gives them lands there, thus creating Philistia. The Hittite Empire disintegrates under this same pressure, combined with the

Slate palette, dated pre-3100 B.C., illustrating Egyptians armed with the double-convex bow, in which the distance between bowstring and centre of bow was reduced, enabling the archer to obtain a longer pull, creating greater tension and range. The light troops of the Old Kingdom used such a bow. (Author's collection)

growth of Assyrian power. The Phrygians arrive from the northwest to take over the lands of the Hittites in Asia Minor, while Assyria seizes Mesopotamia and establishes the Early Empire, which lasts until 885.

1200–1100 During this century the great Egyptian Empire also declines as the Pharaohs lose authority over their generals. With the great empires gone or in decline, and Assyria not yet at the height of its power, the various peoples in Palestine and Syria coalesce into a number of independent and constantly warring states. Notable amongst these are the Philistines and Phoenicians (the Greek name for the Canaanites) in the coastal plain of Syria and Palestine; the Israelites in the hills of Palestine; the Aramaean kingdoms of eastern Syria—of which Damascus was the most important; and the Ammonites, Moabites, Midianites and Edomites east and south of the Jordan and the Dead Sea.

1116–1093 *Assyria:* Assyria becomes the leading power in the Middle East.

1110 *Mesopotamia:* End of classical period of Elam, followed by 300 years of silence.

1100 *Egypt:* End of Egyptian Empire, following a century of decline as military caste dispute central authority of the Pharaoh and split empire into a number of independent feudal states.

1080–1025 *Palestine:* Israel invaded by Philistines and subjugated by them.

1028–1013 *Palestine:* Israelites under Saul defeat and expel Philistines.

1010–973 *Palestine:* Israelites under David check and destroy resurgent Philistine power. United Monarchy of Israel and Judah formed, and becomes involved in continuous wars with Edom, Ammon, and Moab, and Aramaeans to the north. United Monarchy conquers Palestine and dominates most of Syria, creating an empire extending from the border of Egypt to the Euphrates.

950 *Egypt:* Libyans overrun Egypt and found XXII (Libyan) Dynasty (950–730), but are eventually absorbed into Egyptian society and culture.

950–929 *Palestine:* Egyptian campaigns against United Monarchy.

925 *Palestine:* Following death of Solomon (933), and after long wars with Egypt, Judah and Israel are divided. There follow 20 years of war between the two states, and with their neighbours.

885–859 *Assyria:* Reign of Ashurnasirpal II: capital moved to Nimrud.

Arrow heads of the Late Bronze Age, *circa* **14th century B.C. Egyptian arrows were of wood or reed with feather flights. Quivers were of leather or basketry, and held 20 to 30 arrows. (By courtesy of the Israel Dept of Antiquities and Museums)**

879 *Mesopotamia:* Ashurnasirpal II defeats Kassites at Suru.

876 *Palestine:* Building of Israelite capital at Samaria.

858–824 *Assyria:* Repeated campaigns by Shalmaneser III to subdue Aramaeans.

852 *Palestine:* Moabites re-establish independence from Israel.

835 *Mesopotamia:* Migration of Medes into what is now north-west Iran, Kurdistan and Azerbaijan. Clash with Assyrians.

821 *Mesopotamia:* Elamites conquered by Assyrians.

818 *Mesopotamia:* Assyrians defeat alliance of Babylonians, Elamites and Chaldeans at Dur-Papsukal.

799–785 *Palestine:* Judah regains independence and takes Edom.

751 *Egypt:* Birth of new kingdom of Ethiopia with capital at Napata. The kings subsequently rule Egypt (XXV Ethiopian Dynasty) until 656.

745–727 *Assyria:* Reign of Tiglath-pileser III, who founds the Late or Neo-Assyrian Empire. Invades Palestine and Syria, and also wages war on Babylonians, Arabs and Medes.

742 *Mesopotamia:* Elamites revolt against Assyrian rule, and also fight off Persians encroaching from east.

722 *Palestine:* Samaria taken by Assyrians. Large part of population deported to remote parts of Assyrian Empire: survivors are mixed with imported Syrians, Arabs and Babylonians and subsequently become the Samaritans.

Bronze 'epsilon' axe-head, riveted to a silver haft, of the type used by heavy infantry of the Middle Kingdom. This method of fixing head to haft was sufficient for those armies which did not have to fight armoured enemies, but in Mesopotamia the Sumerians developed a narrow-bladed piercing axe to deal with their armoured enemies, and this was fastened to the haft more securely by a pipe-like socket cast at right angles to the rear of the blade. (British Museum)

Israel ceases to exist.

721–705 *Assyria:* Reign of Sargon II: capital moved to Khorsabad.

706 *Mesopotamia:* All Chaldean cities now under Assyrian domination.

705–680 *Assyria:* Reign of Sennacherib: capital moved to Nineveh.

701–699 *Syria:* Babylon revolts against Assyrian rule and allies with Philistine cities, Judah, Edom, Moab, Ammon and Egypt, but at Altaqu (Eltekeh) the allies are defeated by Sennacherib, who then invades Judah and sacks Lachish.

700 *Mesopotamia:* Assyria gains dominance over Medes.

690 *Mesopotamia:* Alliance of Elamites, Aramaeans and Chaldeans defeated by Assyrians at Khalule.

689 *Mesopotamia:* Babylon sacked by Sennacherib.

690–681 *Palestine:* Pharaoh Taharqa (690–664) checks Assyrians, forces Sennacherib to retire from Judah, and restores Egyptian influence in Syria.

674 *Palestine:* Assyrian advance on Egypt forced back.

671 *Egypt:* Assyrians invade Egypt and take Memphis.

668–661 *Egypt:* Series of Egyptian revolts, aided by Greek mercenaries and under the Saite or XXVI Dynasty (663–525). Suppressed by Assyrians. Thebes sacked in 663.

9

Egyptian troops of the New Kingdom (1567–1085), based on wall paintings at Thebes. The heavy infantry are now armoured, with smaller shields and secondary weapons which include short swords and a new form of axe. Archers equipped with the composite bow are at the left. (From Wilkinson)

652 *Mesopotamia :* Another Babylonian revolt suppressed by Assyrians.

640 *Mesopotamia :* Elamite revolt crushed by Ashurbanipal.

640–626 *Assyria :* Assyrians crush further revolts by Arabs and Elamites, but are seriously weakened; when Ashurbanipal, last of the great Assyrian kings, dies in 630 the Scythian tribes begin to cross the northern frontier at will, ravaging the disintegrating empire.

628–609 *Palestine :* As Assyrian power declines, Judah expands to incorporate much of former Israel.

626 *Mesopotamia :* Babylon, assisted by the Medes, revolts once more. Start of Neo-Babylonian Empire under Chaldean Dynasty of Nabopolassar (625–605).

614 *Assyria :* Ashur taken by Medes.

612 *Assyria :* Nineveh destroyed by Babylonians and Medes. Assyrian empire divided between Babylon (all land west of Tigris) and Media (all land east of Tigris). The two-thousand-year-old Assyrian people are all but wiped from the face of the earth; the destruction of them and their capital being so complete that when Xenophon passed Nineveh two centuries later he and his army were oblivious to its existence.

The Peoples

The Sumerians

The origins of the Sumerians are unknown: the portraits of themselves which they have left behind show them to have been unlike any other people in the Middle East, or indeed the world. We know only that they were a non-Semitic race which sometime before 3500 B.C. founded a collection of city-states known as Sumer. The earliest and most significant of these cities was Uruk, of which the legendary Gilgamesh was once king. Around 2800, when at its height, Uruk had a population of some 40,000 and was surrounded by 146 villages. Kish, Ur, Eshnunna, Umma, Khafaje, Lagash and Nippur were other such city-states, founded between 3500 and 2500. These cities were constantly at war with each other, until first united *circa* 2500 under a king from Ur.

The Sumerians were the first to introduce bronze into warfare, and were centuries ahead of the Egyptians in the use of the wheel. Our two most important sources for their fighting forces are the Standard of Ur and the Stele of Vultures, both dated at around 2500 B.C. Both show that the Sumerians were the first to use war chariots and infantry phalanx, apparently in close harmony.

Their chariots were four-wheeled and of heavy construction. Traction was by four onagers—wild asses—so it is doubtful if the chariot moved very quickly: modern experiments have shown that a speed of 15mph was possible, though the chariot could only make a wide turn at this speed. However, it was not intended for rapid manoeuvring in the Egyptian style, but for crashing through the ranks of the enemy, the main weapons of the charioteers being javelins and spears.

The infantry were protected by large shields and bronze helmets, some also wearing a heavy cloak studded with metal. Covered by their shields, these infantrymen advanced in phalanx formation, their spears held with both hands and thrust forward horizontally. The Sumerian artists illustrate this phalanx in a stylized form, but it would appear to be in column of six files with 11 men in each file—possibly ten men and a file leader. By a simple left or right turn this column could become a phalanx 11 files wide by six ranks deep, a unit of 60 men plus officers. This early phalanx was remarkable for the discipline and organization required to create it but, lacking an archer force to support their spearmen and chariots, the Sumerians were defeated with comparative ease by their successors, the Akkadians, who fielded large numbers of archers.

The army of Sumer was formed from contingents from each of the city states, under a system of hereditary obligation: e.g. Lagash, *circa* 2400 had a population of around 30,000 and had to provide 20 chariots and 1,000 infantry.

The Akkadians

The Semites in Mesopotamia were originally known collectively as Akkadians because of their 'empire' centred on Akkad, but soon after 2000 B.C. the Semites in the south became known as the Babylonians because of their establishment of a kingdom at Babylon: those in the west were now Amorites, while those in the north-west were now known as the Assyrians.

The army of Sargon (*circa* 2350) is supposed to have contained 5,400 men. It was a citizen army, composed entirely of light troops, many of whom were archers. At least some of the archers appear to have been armed with the composite bow. This strong archer force probably explains why the

Models of Egyptian spearmen, from the tomb of Mesehti. Shields of the Old Kingdom were rectangular, the shape shown here not appearing until *circa* 2000 B.C. Such large shields, of wood covered with hide, were necessary because of the lack of body defences; but their weight slowed the men down, and a smaller, lighter shield of the same shape began to appear in the Middle Kingdom period. (Egyptian Museum, Cairo)

Akkadians were able to defeat the Sumerians, who relied on javelins and hand-to-hand fighting for victory.

The Babylonians

There is little information available on the early Babylonian Empire, but we do know that until the time of Hammurabi (*circa* 1764–1725) the main army consisted of levies, with a small royal guard. Hammurabi's own royal guard (probably synonymous with professional or regular troops) is said to have contained between 10,000 and 20,000 men. It was probably much larger than those of his predecessors. The men appear to have been slaves or mercenaries, men less likely to be corrupted by internal intrigues.

Hammurabi was also responsible for instituting a feudal system, whereby citizens (*amelov*) were granted land in return for a pledge to serve in the army in the field or on garrison duty whenever needed. In return the king undertook to provide a substitute to look after the land when the *amelov* was away on service. The land grants eventually became hereditary, and the *amelov* provided the main part of all Babylonian armies.

In the 900–626 period it has to be assumed that the citizen army remained as before, with the royal bodyguard still recruited from outside the empire (it included Elamites and men of the Sutu desert tribes). The army now had three arms—infantry, cavalry and chariots, with the emphasis on mounted troops and the bow, the Babylonians being renowned for their skill with that weapon:

Egyptian troops of the XVIII Dynasty (1567–1320). (From Wilkinson)

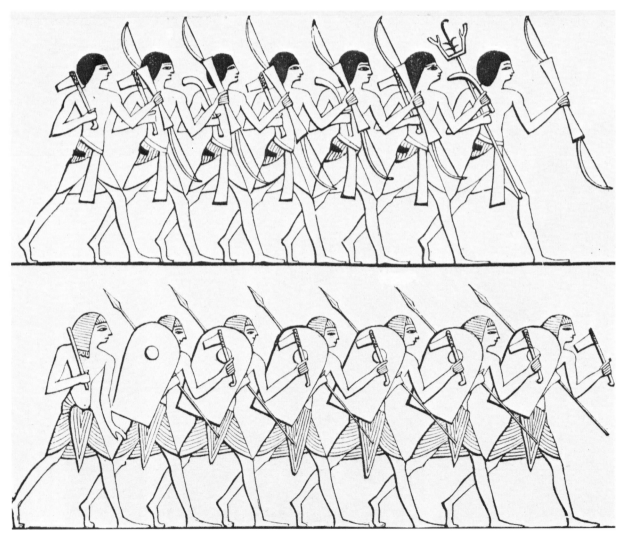

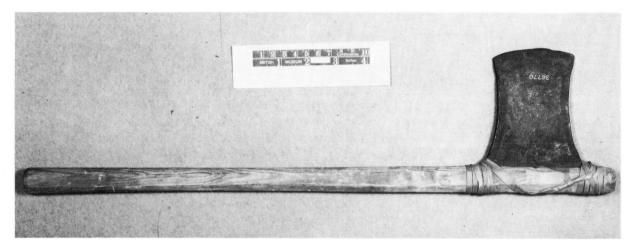

almost all the mounted men and the larger part of the infantry were so armed. The royal guard probably had 600 cavalry and at least 4,000 infantry.

The actual strength of the army is difficult to assess, as in most battles the Babylonians were assisted by allies. At Dur-Papsukal (818) the Babylonians and Chaldeans, together with their Elamite allies, lost 13,000 killed and 3,000 taken prisoner, yet a second army was able to fight the Assyrians shortly afterwards, losing a further 5,000 men, 200 horses and 100 chariots. After the battle of Kutha (706) the Assyrians had conquered all the Chaldean cities, and their army returned home with 208,000 prisoners and 7,200 horses—the city of Sarrabani alone yielded 55,000 prisoners when it fell in 713. Finally, at Khalule (690), an alliance of Chaldeans, Elamites and Aramaeans was defeated with a loss of 150,000 killed, according to the Assyrians. Discounting exaggeration, allied troops and non-combatants included in the above figures, it is obvious the Babylonians could field very large armies—certainly up to 50,000 men.

The Elamites

The Elamites are first mentioned in Sumerian documents dated *circa* 2680 B.C., although there is archaeological evidence of their existence as early as at least 3000 B.C. They did not emerge as a major power, with their capital at Susa, until the late 13th–early 12th century. Their land is today known as Khuzistan, a mainly mountainous region in southwest Iran, 'Elam' being a Semitic translation of the original name of Numma, 'Highlands'.

Bronze axe bearing the name Thutmose III. This is a typical axe of the period, with much narrower cutting edge to pierce armour, but still lacking a socket. (British Museum)

The Elamites were probably a mixture of Semites, infiltrating the area from the west from the 25th century onwards, and dark-skinned aboriginals of uncertain race. The modern Lurs, a tall mountain people with brown skin and black hair, probably resemble closely the ancient Elamites.

The first mention of Elamite military forces occurs *circa* 2100 B.C., when an Elamite 'foreign legion' was recruited by the Sumerians to reinforce garrisons and guard the frontier on the Zagros Mountains against migrating peoples. These 'border guards' worked in groups of five to 25 men, and existed on a daily ration of barley-bread and ale. The next mentions are in the 13th century, when Elam mustered 3,415 'horned warriors' to send to Huhnur: it is usually assumed these warriors wore horned helmets, and this casts doubt on Rameses II's Sherden mercenaries, who may have been Elamites after all! They also provided 12,000 (1,200 would be a more likely figure) warriors for the bodyguard of the Hittite king at Hattusas.

Most of our information dates from the late 8th and early 7th centuries, when Elam was involved with Babylon in the wars against Assyria. For example in 710 there were 7,500 Elamites involved in the defence of the cities of Samuna and Bab-Duri, and an alleged 80,000 archers and some cavalry at the battle of Kutha (706). Following the usual convention for dealing with ancient exaggeration, we get a figure of 8,000 archers, which is

Royal princes of the New Kingdom. Princes were identified by a 'badge' hanging from the side of the head which enclosed or represented the lock of hair worn by all children. The princes retained this symbolic lock during the lifetime of their father to indicate that they had not arrived at kinghood. (From Wilkinson)

feasible. At a battle in 703, again with Babylon against the Assyrians, Elam fielded a strong force of bowmen and cavalry. It would appear from this, and other references to the Elamites, that they were renowned as archers, while Assyrian reliefs of the period show their forces to be almost exclusively bow-armed and unarmoured. The bulk of their forces were on foot, but there were some cavalry and chariots: amongst the plunder taken by Ashurbanipal at Susa in 646 were 'the chariots of triumph and of war decorated with gold and electron, the horses and mules with their gold and silver trappings . . .' The Elamites followed the Sumerian, Hittite and later Assyrian practice of developing heavy war carts, as well as the light chariot; it may be that the horses hauled the chariots and the mules the war carts.

According to Sennacherib, the élite Elamite warriors were distinguished by 'golden daggers and heavy rings of shining gold on their wrists'.

In 691 the Elamite army also contained 'warriors from Parzuash'—the first appearance in Elamite history of the people from 'the land of the Persians', on the eastern border of Elam.

The Egyptians

In the Old Kingdom each *nome*, or tribe, had its own militia, presumably based on some form of short military service as youths came of age, followed by a muster of the appropriate number of trained men whenever they were needed. Therefore, the army of the Pharaoh at this time consisted almost entirely of contingents of militia from those nomes in the Nile valley which recognized the Pharaoh at Memphis as their warlord. The Pharaoh and governors of the nomes probably had small bodyguards which would have formed the nucleus of the army.

The Kingdom's army was commanded by the vizier, and there was a 'director of arsenals' to supply weapons, equipment and food to the soldiers, and a 'director of infantry' whose job was presumably to see to their organization and training, and to deal with other staff work. The army consisted entirely of infantry, divided into light and heavy troops.

Mercenaries were recruited from Nubia, and later Libya, to provide a larger army when necessary, and towards the end of the kingdom a great percentage of the army consisted of such mercenaries, probably because the militia tended to be more loyal to the nomes, at the expense of royal or national interests.

The army of the Theban princes of the Middle Kingdom avoided the mistakes of its predecessors by recruiting a strong Egyptian element. Each nome still had to provide a quota of recruits, but now they entered into permanent military service under the Pharaoh, and were so completely isolated from the rest of the population that they became known as 'those who live in the army', or 'followers of His Majesty'. For example, the city of Apu (the Panopolis of the Greeks) had to supply 600 infantry for service in the Pharaoh's army, and when these men were marched away by the Pharaoh's representatives they were mourned as if dead, for it was known they would never be seen in Apu again. To encourage an *esprit de corps* in their armies, the Pharaohs lavishly rewarded gallant service in the field with presentations of daggers of honour and golden collars.

Mercenaries were also recruited, again from Nubia and Libya, but this time their numbers were not allowed to become too great, and they were frequently given policing and garrison duties so that their strength was divided, whilst that of the native contingents was concentrated in the main army. The Pharaoh also had a small royal bodyguard.

The army was entirely infantry, divided into heavy spearmen of the phalanx, and the archers, probably about fifty per cent of each. It can be assumed from information in the Bible and various monuments that the organization of the army was based on the decimal system, the strengths of the various units being listed as 100, 600, 1,000, 2,000 and 3,000. The last two probably represented a 'corps' or expeditionary force. There was also a 300-strong group used as an assault unit, divided into three 'companies' each of 100 men. Other documents of the 18th century refer to militia units of 10,000 warriors, but these were presumably the local troops of the various nomes or provincial

Egyptian chariot of the New Kingdom, drawn in perspective and designed from a comparison of different sculptures. (From Wilkinson)

districts: the strength of the Pharaoh's *standing army* probably did not exceed 10,000 to 13,000 men at most, and it is quite possible that even at this early date the army may have been divided into two 'divisions' of 5,000 men, with the balance in the Pharaoh's bodyguard. It is known that prior to about 1300 there were two divisions in the army, named after gods—thus the Amun Division, named after the supreme deity of Egypt, and the Re Division, named after the sun god—and it is also known that the 600 infantry from Apu served in the Amun Division.

Models of soldiers from this period show that both spearmen and archers marched in disciplined formations, four abreast, and it is certain therefore that they also fought in organized formations suited to their different rôles.

The new army which arose after the expulsion of the Hyksôs (see below) was of a revolutionary form, for the Hyksôs had not only introduced new weapons and equipment (scale armour and the composite bow) but had also brought with them the chariot. Therefore, the armies of the New Kingdom for the first time had a mounted arm to support the spear phalanx and archer units.

As under the Middle Kingdom, each nome was still responsible for supplying a contingent for the Pharaoh's regular army, which was for the most part Egyptian. However, after a period of service in the army, the men returned to their nomes and others took their place, thus creating a trained reservist force. Further details about the armies of the early kings of this period are not known, but we do know that at the time of Haremheb (1340–1320), there were still only two divisions. As the new empire grew so did the army: Seti I (1318–1298) added a third division (named after Set, god of violence), and Rameses II added a fourth (named after Ptah, the god who created the world). Sometime after 1288 a fifth division was added, named after Phra, the incarnation of Re.

Certain cities and districts of Egypt were appropriated to certain gods, who were the chief deities of the place: Amun's principal temple was at Thebes, Memphis was the great city of Ptah, Heliopolis was the city of the sun god Re, Set appears to have originated in the Delta under the Hyksôs, and so on. As no two neighbouring districts, or chief cities, were given to the same god, it is possible that the various divisions were made up entirely of men recruited from the cities and districts of the gods after whom the divisions were named, though this is pure conjecture.

By this date (late 14th–early 13th centuries) we know that each nome had an active and reserve military force; the active force providing the quota for the Pharaoh's army and a local force, relieved turn and turn about by the reserve force. It is quite likely this system existed from the beginning of the New Kingdom.

Organization of the regular army was again on the decimal system. Using modern terms there was, from at least the beginning of the 14th century, a section of ten men with an NCO; a platoon of 40 men with NCOs and a junior officer; a company of four or five platoons, perhaps 200–250 men; and a battalion (Pdt) of four or five companies totalling around 500 men, commanded by a 'Commander of the Host'. Ten such hosts or battalions formed a division, commanded by a general or prince and named after one of the gods. Thus an expeditionary force sent to crush rebels at Djahi consisted of 5,000 men (not including their officers), while the king of Byblos, pleading with the Pharaoh for help to save his city from enemy attacks, requested an expeditionary force of 5,000 men and 50 chariots. For the Megiddo (1468) and Arvad (1472) campaigns, Thutmose III had armies of between 15,000 and 20,000 (three or four divisions); at Kadesh (1288) Rameses II had four divisions of 5,000 men each; and at Perire (1227) Merneptah also had at least 20,000 troops. Peacetime strength was 10,000 men, wartime strength 20,000 as indicated, but with the 20,000 reservists probably called up to protect Egypt whilst the active force was away.

The Pharaoh normally led the army in the field, and his sons held important posts under him, commanding divisions or a wing—called a horn in ancient times. The privileged officer class, which came to rank equal to the priesthood, consisted of *haut, mer, aten* and *menh*, corresponding roughly to the modern general, lieutenant-colonel, captain and lieutenant.

Egyptian phalanx of the New Kingdom, based on wall paintings at Thebes. (From Wilkinson)

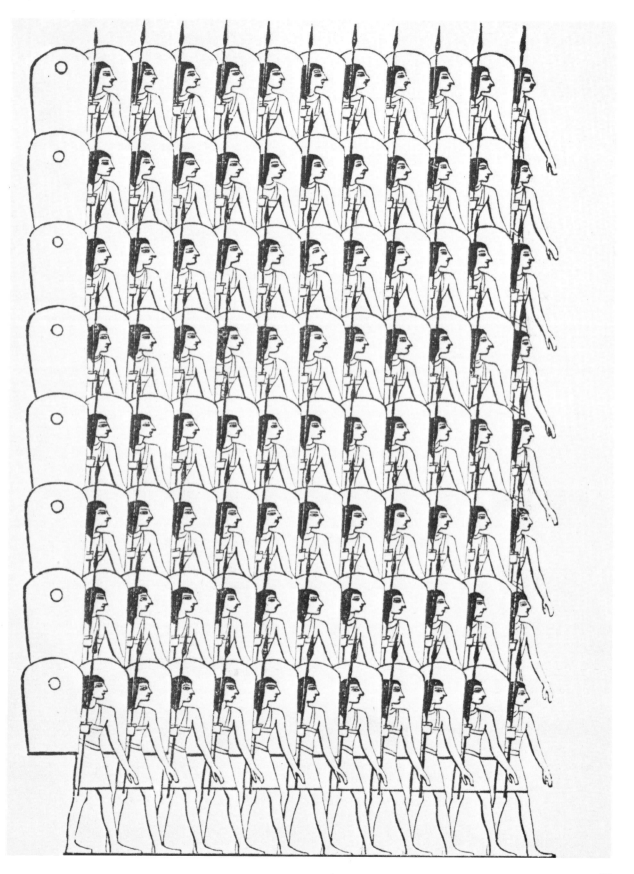

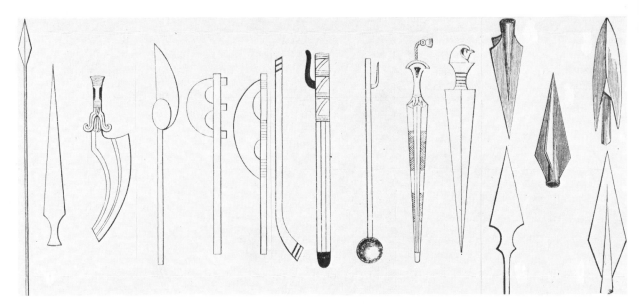

Egyptian weapons, based on archaeological discoveries at Thebes. Left to right: spear, straight sword, *khopesh*, pole-axe, 'eye-axe', 'epsilon axe', hurling stick, two maces, two daggers, and five metal arrow heads, one having small projections from the tang to prevent it splitting the shaft on impact. (From Wilkinson and Rawlinson)

The infantry remained divided into 'battalions' according to weapon, but now included slingers as well as archers and spearmen. The slingers and most archers were light troops, the heavy infantry being the spearmen of the phalanx, with axe or *khopesh* as a secondary weapon. The reliefs commemorating the battle of Kadesh clearly show the formation of the phalanx for the attack: ten ranks deep, the men in each section forming a file, one behind the other. Such a phalanx could march in a column ten men wide, and could easily deploy to either flank by a simple left or right turn, though deployment to front or rear by means of a wheeling manoeuvre would take longer.

The army of Thutmose III (*c.*1490–*c.*1436) was mainly infantry with some chariots incorporated as an integral part of the infantry formations; but a century later the chariots were much more numerous and were organized as a separate arm, though some were normally attached to the infantry divisions, with a large central reserve. Contemporary documents refer to units of 50, 30 and ten chariots, and it would seem the smallest unit was ten, with several such 'troops' grouped to make a 'squadron' of 30 or 50 under a captain. The largest chariot formation is believed to have been

150, or a 'regiment' of three to five 'squadrons', and this was the chariot formation attached to the infantry division. As Sheshonq I (950–929) is said to have had 1,200 chariots when invading Judah (Chronicles (2) XII:3) this would leave some 600, or fifty per cent of the chariotry, as a separate concentrated strike force.

There were few mercenaries in the army at the beginning of the New Kingdom, but as time went on Nubians and Asiatics were added to the infantry —a crack unit of Canaanites, the Na'arun, is mentioned at Kadesh in 1288. Rameses II (1290–1223) is believed to have had Sherden warriors fighting for him against the Hittites in Syria: the Sherden certainly fought for Egypt against their own kind when the Sea Peoples first entered Palestine. After the Sea Peoples had been defeated, Rameses III recruited large numbers of Sherden and Philistine warriors, and also their allies, the Libyans. In time the number of mercenaries became so great that they constituted the backbone of the army, the Sherden forming a large part of the royal bodyguard and, together with the Philistines, providing most of the close-combat troops.

The mercenaries mostly retained their own distinctive dress and weapons, though some were equipped with Egyptian weapons and wore Egyptian dress: all were organized in the Egyptian style. The expeditionary force sent to Djahi reveals just how the Egyptian element in the army had declined in numbers by the XX Dynasty:

totalling 5,000 men, the force consisted of 1,900 archers (presumably Egyptian), 520 Sherden, 1,600 Qeheq Libyans, 100 Meshwesh Libyans, and 880 Nubians. The officers of the mercenaries eventually became a distinct class, and Sheshonq I, founder of the XXII (Libyan) Dynasty, was in fact a Libyan soldier-of-fortune placed on the throne of Egypt by the mercenaries in the Pharaoh's army.

The only information we have on the army of the Late Period (c.1085–525) comes from Herodotus (c.485–425), who gives the total strength of the Egyptian army in his day as 410,000. It has been estimated that in the Late Period the population of Egypt was between five and seven millions, so it was possible for the Pharaohs to have such a large army, but not to keep it constantly under arms. Campaigns were usually short, and it is most likely that the troops were levied only as required and disbanded immediately the crisis was over. They would have required some military training, so there was probably some form of militia, as in earlier times.

Herodotus describes the military strength of Egypt as divided into two distinct armies, the *Hermotykies* and the *Calasiries* (from the original *Klashr*). The *Calasiries* were the most numerous with 250,000 men drawn from the nomes of Thebes, Bubastis, Aphthis, Tanis, Mendes, Sebennytus, Athribis, Pharbaethis, Thmuis, Onuphis, Anyis, and the isle of Myecphoris. All these nomes, with the exception of Thebes, were within the Delta area, and are supposed to have supplied men who were almost all archers. The *Hermotykies* numbered 160,000 and came from Busiris, Sais, Papremis, the isle of Prosopitis, and Natho (again, all regions of the Delta), together with Chemmis in Upper Egypt.

A thousand men from each of these 'armies' served on a rota system in the royal guard, being selected annually. Some others were mustered for garrison duty in a similar way. All other soldiers had to provide their own weapons, equipment and —at least initially—their own rations.

Proportions of troop types are not known, but

Allies and enemies of Egypt in the New Kingdom period. Top row: Phoenician; Syrians with distinctive shields attacking two Hittite chariots. Bottom row: Syrian, Syrian or Canaanite, Canaanite warrior, a group of Nubians and two Kushites. (From Wilkinson)

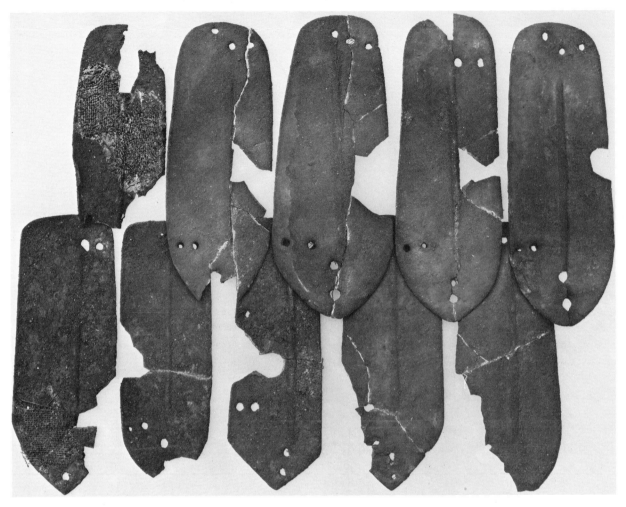

Bronze scales from a 14th century body armour, found in the palace of Amenhotep III in Thebes. Clearly visible are the holes through which the scales were sewn on to a leather or thickly padded fabric coat (parts of which survive at the left), the way the scales were fitted to each other, and the central spine which gave greater strength without increasing weight. The manufacture of scale armour demanded high technical skills: this and the high cost limited the use of scale armour to the rich and technically advanced empires. (Metropolitan Museum of Art, New York)

as we saw earlier, there were at least 1,200 chariots in the 10th century; at the same date there were supposed to be 60,000 cavalry, and infantry without number, including Ethiopians (Chronicles (2) XII:3). The cavalry figure is no doubt an exaggeration, but by following the usual practice of removing a nought we can arrive at the feasible figure of 6,000. It is possible the *Hermotykies* provided the phalanx troops, the *Calasiries* the missile men.

The phalanx of spearmen remained and was apparently both inflexible and indestructible. A 'corps' of 10,000 Egyptian spearmen served in the army of Croesus, king of Lydia (546–540), against the Persians. Drawn up in their standard formation, the Egyptians refused to change formation when Croesus asked them to extend their frontage. In the event, the old Egyptian phalanx proved so formidable that the Persians were unable to break it, even after the rest of Croesus' army had been defeated, and the Persian king finally granted the Egyptians an honourable surrender, giving them the cities of Larissa and Cyllone in which to settle. Their descendants still lived in those cities in the time of Xenophon (430–355).

The Libyans
The Libyans were numerous and warlike, but were normally divided by tribal differences. They are known by a variety of names in Egyptian sources: the Ribu and Libu, or the Tehenu and

Temehu. Later the tribes of Kehek (Qeheq) and Meshwesh are mentioned, these two tribes being particularly noted for their military skill, and serving as mercenaries in the armies of the Pharaohs.

The number of Libyan warriors taking the field at any one time was kept small by the tribal division, but *circa* 3200 the Pharaoh Menes is alleged to have taken 120,000 prisoners when subduing the Libyans. A figure of 12,000 might be acceptable in this context, and shows the Libyans could produce a formidable army when united. In 1227, at the battle of Perire, 20,000 Libyans allied themselves with the Sea Peoples, and in 1193 Rameses III killed or captured 13,500 Libyans.

The Libyan warrior was traditionally a light infantryman, armed simply with bow or spear, but in 1185 Rameses III killed or captured 4,200 Meshwesh warriors, *together with* 93 chariots and 183 horses, which indicates that by this date at least they were importing chariots and horses, and had acquired the skills necessary to use them in battle.

The Nubians and Ethiopians

The Nubians are referred to by the Egyptians as the Nahsior or Nahasu, and were (at least initially) a negro race which inhabited the Nile valley south of the First Cataract, called by the Egyptians the land of Wawat. They were divided into numerous tribes, appear to have been almost entirely naked, and totally rejected all attempts by the Egyptians to subjugate or 'civilize' them. The tribes were scattered and disunited, but constantly raided Egypt despite numerous expeditionary forces sent against them: 7,000 prisoners were taken in one such expedition *circa* 2600.

The Nubians were a martial people, particularly the nomadic Medjway (or Medjai) tribe of the Second Cataract region, but they were never a serious threat to Egypt because of their disunity, while their warriors were armed only with bow or spear. Nubians fought as mercenaries in the Egyptian army from about 2000 B.C., and were particularly valued in the rôle of light archers. The Medjway warriors were recruited in some numbers.

Further south, above the Third Cataract, were the 'vile Kush' or Kesh, who were not negroes but Caucasians, ancestors of the Ethiopians. Both Herodotus and Egyptian monuments segregate the Kush into two main types: a straight-haired race and a woolly-haired race, dwelling to the east and west of the Nile respectively.

Although divided into many tribes, the Kush were considerably more dangerous than the Nubians, and at times controlled the Nile valley along its entire length from Khartoum to the very borders of Egypt. Consequently they were gradually subjugated by the Pharaohs, and in the XVIII Dynasty their land became an Egyptian province, paying tribute in slaves, oxen, gold and ivory. The Kush frequently rebelled and were as often subdued, but they finally regained their independence towards the end of the 11th century

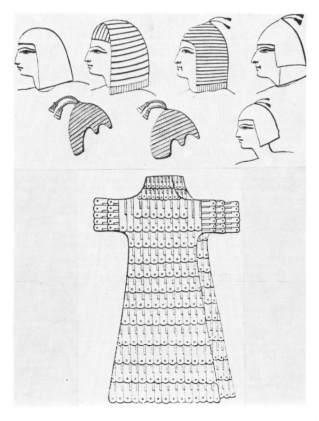

Egyptian scale armour (from the tomb of Rameses III) and a variety of protective head gear of the same period. It is believed most Egyptian head defences were of thick, padded fabric (often coloured green, red or black), for no example of a metal helmet has survived or been found in a painting or relief. However, some heavy infantry *may* have worn bronze helmets, covered by an insulating material which was also decorative, and the prestige value of such helmets is clearly shown in wall paintings of the period—bronze helmets are illustrated in the hands of Semites (Canaanites?) bearing tribute. (From Wilkinson and Rawlinson)

21

and formed a united kingdom with its capital at Napata (modern Merowe). This kingdom grew ever more powerful until in the mid-8th century it conquered Egypt and set up the XXV (Ethiopian) Dynasty. They were expelled by the Egyptians *circa* 660, but continued thereafter as an independent kingdom.

No details of their army are known, but the Kush were a tall, strong and warlike race whose warriors were disciplined and must therefore have fought in organized formations. Because of the nature of their land their army was probably entirely of infantry, possibly heavy spearmen supported by light archers and javelin men.

The Hyksôs

Translation of the word Hyksôs, and consequently identification of the people bearing that name, tends to vary alarmingly: they are variously believed to have been Arabs, Canaanites, and even an Indo-European people from Asia. Modern scholars tend to discount the earlier 'invasion of Egypt' theory, and lean towards a steady build up of power from within the Egyptian Empire, culminating in the setting up of an independent dynasty in Lower Egypt *circa* 1700, while Upper Egypt continued to be ruled by the princes of Thebes.

In the 18th century the Egyptians did not have the chariot or scale armour, and were still using the double-convex bow and a copper axe-blade which had to be lashed into a cleft at the top of the haft. The Hyksôs, however, are still credited by most authorities with the introduction into Egypt of the chariot, the horse, scale armour, the composite bow, bronze swords and axe-heads, the latter having a hole for the haft. Such weapons could not have been introduced into Egypt by a people already within the Empire, but must have come from outside, from a people with a much more advanced technology.

During the 1991–1786 period Egypt had ex-

Bronze dagger with gilt-covered hilt, *circa* 1550–1500, illustrating the transition of a straight-edged cutting weapon from dagger to sword. Such daggers were between 12 and 16 inches long (blades 8–10 inches and 1½ inches wide), carried in a sheath of plain or patterned leather. The first true straight-edged swords—the 30-inch-long iron ones of the Sea Peoples—did not materialize until about 1200. (British Museum)

panded south into Nubia and the lower Sudan, and eastwards towards Syria. As the Nubians were the allies of the Hyksôs, the latter must have come from the east, and indeed the often discredited 3rd century B.C. Egyptian historian Manetho does state that Egypt was invaded from the east, by 'ignoble men who conquered the land without a struggle and established their own dynasty of kings at Memphis.' To the east were Arabs, Amorites, and Canaanites, all Semitic peoples, and it is generally accepted that the Hyksôs were of Semitic origin; some experts believe that Hyksôs is nothing more than a collective name for a group of Semitic tribes. The majority of experts interpret Hyksôs as being derived from *Hiku-Shasu* (prince of the desert folk, with *sôs* synonymous with *Shasu*), or *Hik-Khaskhut* (desert prince). However, the Arabs were neither rich enough nor sufficiently advanced to be able to produce chariots, bronze scale-armour and weapons, and the composite bow, though they could have formed a large part of the Hyksôs or Semitic tribes which overran Egypt with such apparent ease: the Egyptians may well have experienced the feeling of helplessness which the Israelites, infantry all, suffered when their kingdom was abruptly and easily overrun by Midianite camel riders in the time of Gideon.

At this date the Egyptians had an army entirely of foot soldiers, unarmoured and equipped with simple weapons—the spear, the double-convex bow, and copper axes. If the Arabs were stiffened by the Canaanites in chariots, wearing scale armour and shooting arrows from composite bows, it would no longer be surprising that the Egyptian Empire was so easily overwhelmed. Manetho appears to confirm this theory when he refers to the XV Dynasty as 'Phoenician' (the Greek name for the Canaanites), and to the XVI Dynasty as originating from Syria. And most historians agree that the chariot came to Egypt from Canaan.

Even at this early date the Canaanites had a rich and advanced civilization: the Canaanite

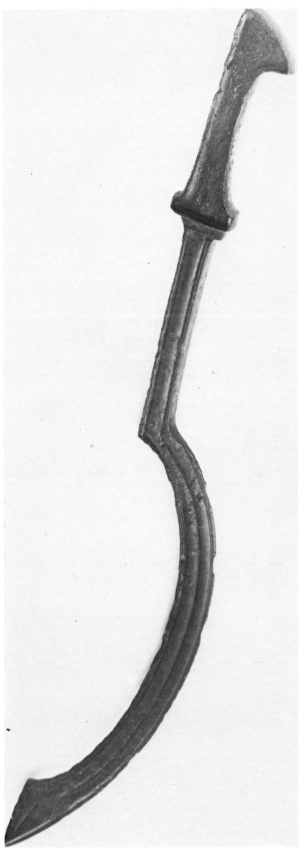

Sickle sword from Canaan, *circa* 1570–1200. By this date the sword had a long blade and short hilt. The Egyptians appear to have learned the art of manufacturing such swords from the Canaanites during the New Kingdom period, and called the swords *khopesh* after their term for the foreleg of an animal. The *khopesh* was still being used by the Egyptians when they fought the Sea Peoples. (Arkeoloji Müzeleri Müdürlüğü, Istanbul)

army at Megiddo (1468), with allied Syrian tribes, numbered between 10,000 and 15,000 men, and the Egyptian booty after the battle included 924 chariots, 2,238 horses, and 200 suits of armour. After their defeat the Canaanites paid tribute in chariots, gold and silver—all symbolic of a rich and technically advanced civilization, and in the 12th–11th-century wars with the Israelites they could still field an army including 900 chariots.

The Hittites

The Hittites were a non-Semitic people from the mountains of Armenia who spread westwards into Asia Minor sometime towards the end of the second millennium B.C. At first divided into independent tribes, they were gradually united under one king who built a great walled city at Hattusas (modern Boghazköy) for their capital.

In the 19th century they occur for the first time in the Bible, as the children of Heth, who dwelt at Hebron in Palestine. At this date the Hittite Empire did not extend so far south, and it is possible that independent groups of Hittites, perhaps resenting unification, had pushed south into Syria and Palestine to establish their own petty kingdoms.

By the mid-16th century the Empire had expanded southwards into Syria and beyond to menace the kingdom of Mitanni and Egypt's position in Palestine. Thutmose III waged 17 campaigns in Syria and the deserts to the east, and ultimately defeated the Hittites; but their pressure southwards started again in the reign of Amenhotep III (1397–1360) and came to a climax during the reign of Amenhotep IV (1370–1353), with Egypt's vassals in the region beginning to change sides. By the time of the death of Tutankhamun (1343) they had gained control of both Syria and Palestine, as well as the kingdom of Mitanni, so that their empire now ranged from Armenia in the north to Palestine in the south, and from the coast of Asia Minor in the west to the Euphrates in the east.

This fantastic growth, despite an unexpectedly sturdy resistance on the part of the Egyptian Empire, owed much to the Hittites' use of iron weapons. Iron tools and weapons had been known in Egypt and Mesopotamia since at least 2700 B.C. (the Sumerians called iron 'metal from heaven', i.e. in meteoric form), but such items were costly and difficult to produce in quantity. However, sometime around 1400 B.C. the Hittites, or a vassal tribe within their empire, discovered a process for producing good quality iron in bulk. The process was kept secret by the Hittites, enabling them to gain an immense advantage over their enemies, who were still using bronze weapons. At this date iron was more valuable than gold, so possession of iron weapons also added great prestige: an Egyptian Pharaoh asked the Hittite king for iron following the treaty between the empires after Kadesh, but received only a single iron dagger. Such a dagger was found amongst the gold and other precious objects in Tutankhamun's fabulous tomb.

The invasions of the Sea Peoples in the late 13th century helped to disperse the ironsmiths, and in due course spread their knowledge throughout the Middle East. The same invasions, coupled with internal disputes and pressure from a growing Assyria, led to the loss of the Hittite capital and eventually the empire, as the Phrygians moved into Asia Minor from the west. However, the Hittites did not disappear entirely, but contracted in, or close to, northern Syria, setting up independent petty kingdoms at Carchemish, Hamath, Malatia, Zinjirli and a number of other places, some of which were soon conquered by the Aramaeans. Here the Hittites survived until the 8th century when they were finally annexed by the Assyrians—Zinjirli in 724, Hamath in 720, and finally Carchemish, the largest city of all, in 717. With the fall of Carchemish the Hittites disappeared from history.

Although the Hittite Empire was controlled by one king, the early days of the petty kingdoms seem never to have been forgotten, and the king always had to humour the feudal nobility which had descended from these kings, and which had an 'assembly of the great'. Under these nobles each province of the empire was administered by a feudal system, under which land and civil concessions were granted in return for military service, for tribute and military assistance in the case of vassal states.

We know that the king had a royal bodyguard, which included 12,000 (more probably 1,200) Elamites. The total strength of the bodyguard is

1. Sumerian heavy infantryman, c.2500 B.C.
2. Egyptian heavy infantryman, 19th Dynasty
3. Egyptian archer, 19th Dynasty

A

Sumerian chariot of King Eannatum of Lagash, c.2500 B.C.

B

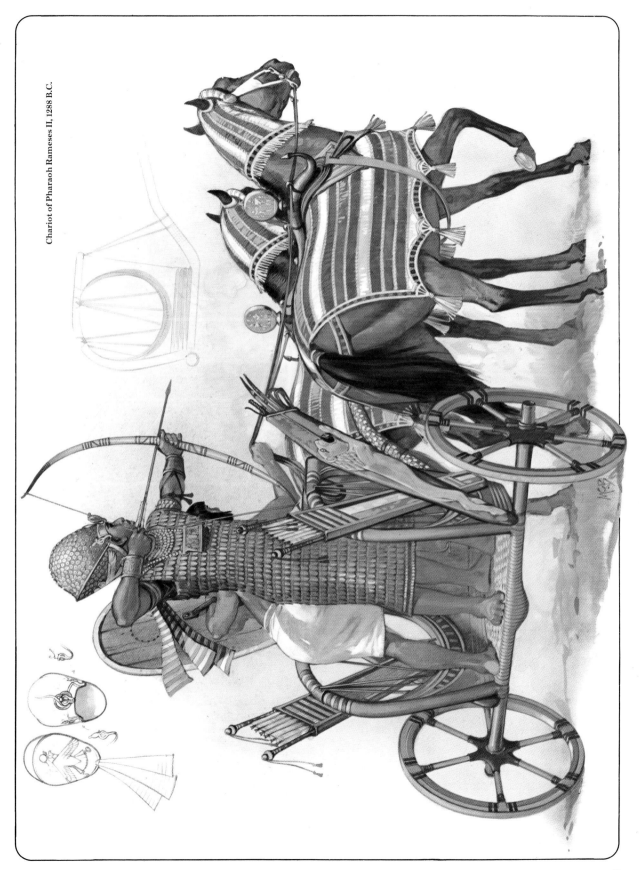

Chariot of Pharaoh Rameses II, 1288 B.C.

C

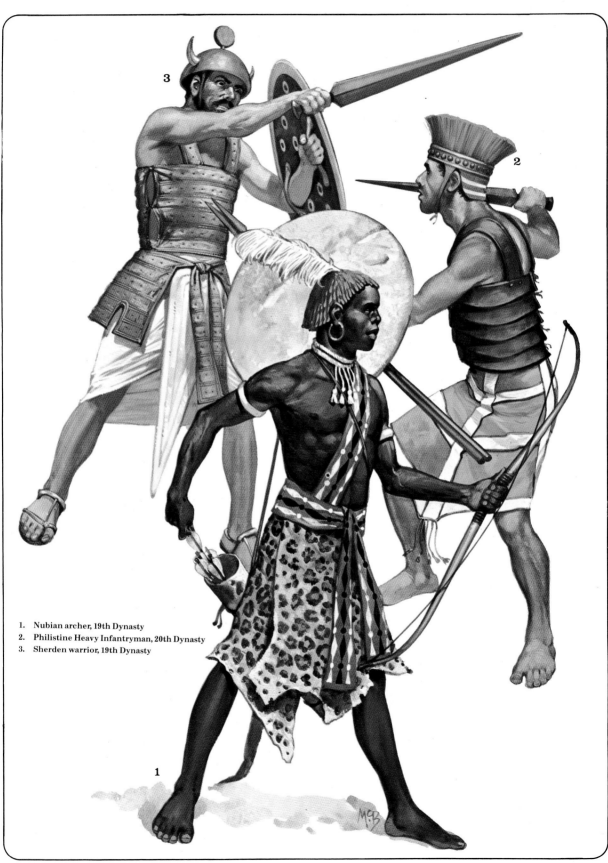

1. Nubian archer, 19th Dynasty
2. Philistine Heavy Infantryman, 20th Dynasty
3. Sherden warrior, 19th Dynasty

D

1. Semite archer, 12th Dynasty
2. Shasu–Bedouin warrior, 19th Dynasty
3. Libyan archer, 20th Dynasty

E

1. Syrian archer, 18th Dynasty
2. Hittite charioteer, 13th century B.C.
3. Hittite warrior, Royal Guard, 9th century B.C.

F

1. Assyrian infantryman, 7th century B.C.
2. Assyrian archer, 8th century B.C.
3. Elamite archer, 7th century B.C.

G

Assyrian mounted archer, Arab camel riders, 7th century B.C.

H

not known, but as some form of standing army was essential for garrison duties it is probable that the guard numbered several thousands of mercenaries and formed the entire standing army, all other troops being levied under the feudal system when required; and then only in those areas actually threatened or involved in border expansion.

The largest army ever raised by the empire was for the campaign ending in the battle of Kadesh, where there were 3,500 chariots and 8,000 to 9,000 infantry, though there were present contingents from every possible ally and vassal. With three men in a chariot, this gives a total of at least 18,500 men, more than half of whom were mounted. It would appear from their tactics that the Hittites relied on this large chariot force for their main attack, the infantry being merely a supporting force. At least fifty per cent of the infantry were Hittite spearmen formed in phalanx, but the remainder were mercenary archers, light troops capable of moving quickly, many of them being recruited from the Sutu desert tribes.

We know of 30 and 100 chariot units in Asia Minor, and of 50 chariots under the command of a 'captain of 50'. This suggests the chariots were organized much like those of the Egyptians, with a 'troop' of ten, a 'squadron' of 30 or 50, and a 'regiment' of perhaps only 100. The crews fought as mounted archers, but they were more akin to mounted infantry, and could be used for close combat either mounted or dismounted. The spearmen were organized in a phalanx much like that of the Egyptians, with a ten-man section forming a file in combat, a rank when in column.

The later petty kingdoms rarely united and were easily crushed by the Assyrians. Hamath, one of the larger kingdoms, did join with Damascus to fight Shalmaneser III at Qarqar in 853, where it fielded 700 chariots, 700 light cavalry, and 10,000 infantry; while after the fall of Carchemish, Sargon formed a contingent of 50 chariots, 200 cavalry and 3,000 infantry from the defeated Hittites. These figures give some indication of the size of the armies which other large kingdoms might have fielded, and indicate proportions of troop types.

The Sea Peoples
The Sea Peoples were a number of different tribes caught up in the mass migratory movements provoked by widespread famine at the end of the 13th century, and possibly also by the movement of the Dorian Greeks into Thessaly and Boeotia in the 12th century, followed by their conquest of Argos, the Achaean kingdoms, Mycenae and Corinth. The most famous of the tribes were the Peleset or Philistines, who seem also to have been the most numerous, and the Sherden. Other known tribes were the Shekelesh, Lukka (Lycians), Teresh, Tjekker, Tyrsenoi, Thekel, Denyen, Weshesh, Teukroi, Akawasha and Zakkaru.

For many years it has been supposed that most if not all of these peoples came from Sicily, Sardinia, Crete and the Peloponnese, migrating through and along the coast of Asia Minor and the Hittite Empire until halted by the Egyptian Empire in Palestine. Rameses III, who defeated them, describes them only as 'the foreign countries made a conspiracy in their islands' and 'their confederation was the Philistines, Tjekker, Shekelesh, Denyen and Weshesh lands united'. That it was a migratory movement and not a military invasion is confirmed by the large numbers of women and children shown accompanying the warriors of these tribes.

Modern authorities now tend to reject these earlier interpretations, and believe the tribes came from the western and southern coasts of Asia Minor and their associated islands; still literally sea peoples, but *not* migrating across the sea, merely displaced by famine and/or pressure from the changing population of Greece and her islands. It is now thought that Teresh and Denyen were probably the two Cilician cities on the south coast of Asia Minor mentioned in Hittite sources as Tarsa and Adaniya; that Akawasha is probably Ahhiyawa in south-west Asia Minor; and that the Sherden are much more likely to have been associated with Cyprus than Sardinia. Similarly, the Peleset, Shekelesh and Tjekker peoples are now associated with the Lukka people from the Pamphylian area of Asia Minor.

The first major clash between the Sea Peoples and the Egyptian Empire seems to have been in the last quarter of the 13th century when some 5,000 of the Sea Peoples were killed or captured by the Pharaoh Merneptah. In 1193 Rameses III again defeated them, inflicting 13,500 casualties, and repeated his success three years later in the great naval and land battles illustrated in the reliefs at Medinet Habu.

However, the Sea Peoples were not crushed by these defeats and Rameses III wisely used them to garrison, and later settle, the cities on the crucial coastal plain of Palestine, thus protecting Egypt's trade routes to the north. Here the Peleset (from which name is derived Palestine) flourished as the Egyptian Empire declined, forming a league of five great cities; Ashkelon, Ashdod, Gaza, Ekron and Gath.

During their migration through the disintegrating Hittite Empire the Philistines appear either to have learnt the iron-manufacturing process, or to have brought south with them ironsmiths from that empire. Certainly they were the first people in what had been Canaan to have iron weapons and armour, and they ensured that over the years they maintained this advantage by prohibiting the trade of ironsmith outside their own cities. 'Now there was no smith found throughout all the land of Israel: for the Philistines said, lest the Hebrews make them swords or spears.' By about 1050 the growth of Philistia was threatening the very existence of Israel, and the Hebrew tribes united under Saul and David to defeat the Philistines.

The Sea Peoples were notable warriors, and it is possible that Rameses II (1290–1223) may have had some Sherden in his army as mercenaries (but see also under Elamites). The Sherden certainly fought for Egypt against their own people and other Sea Peoples in 1190, and were subsequently recruited in considerable numbers for the royal guard and as an élite assault force for close combat. The Philistines were also recruited as mercenaries, again as close-combat troops: they are shown in the reliefs fighting and marching in groups of four, a handy sub-unit for sword fighting, where you need a friend to watch your back and your flanks. Only the Teukroi people appear to have used chariots at this date, armed with bow and/or spear, so that the majority of the Sea Peoples' army was infantry, very few of whom appear to have been armed with the bow.

By the time they fought the Israelites the Philistines were a completely different people, having been settled in cities for some 150 years. Their army by this date consisted of a small force of chariots, each with a three-man crew in the Hittite fashion, and light and heavy infantry armed mainly with two spears and a sword. Their numbers at this date are unknown.

The Arabs

The ancient Arabs were a Semitic people, originally composed entirely of nomadic tribes which ranged over the Arabian peninsula east of Palestine and into the modern Syrian Desert. After the break-up of the great Egyptian and Hittite Empires, *circa* 1200–1100 B.C., some of the southern tribes settled in the kingdoms of Edom, Moab, Ammon and Midian. The more northerly tribes remained nomadic.

The Midianites who ravaged Israel in the time of Gideon used camels for their lightning attacks: they were probably unarmoured and equipped only with the bow—light, fast, and using only hit and run tactics. In the 7th century men from the various petty kingdoms fought in the coalition against Assyria; no details of their armies are known but presumably by this date, after some 500

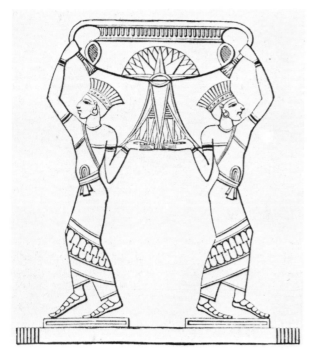

Egyptian vase in the form of two Philistine captives. It is possible that slight differences in the pattern on the band round the helmet shown in various Egyptian works of art were intended to identify the men of the various tribes. (From Wilkinson)

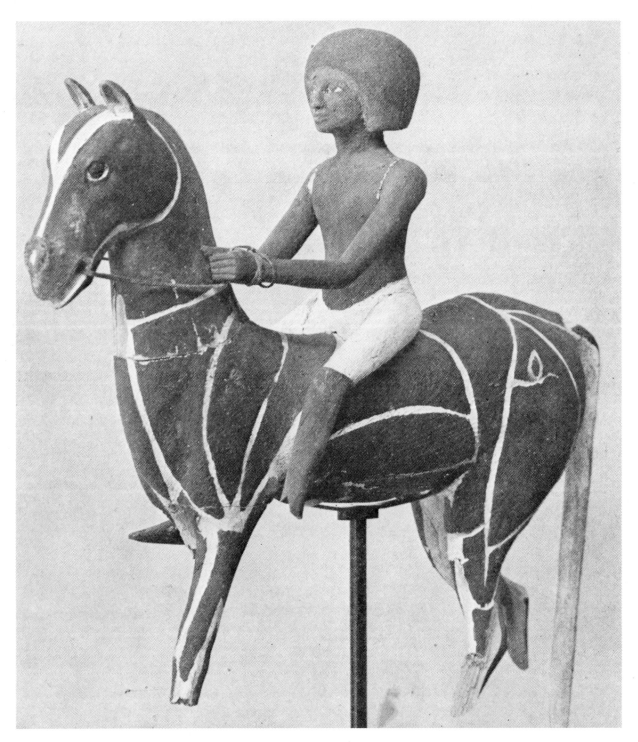

years of settled life, they resembled more those of the Aramaeans (see below).

The nomadic tribes were normally too scattered and independent to become a power in the Middle East, but their warriors could be formidable enemies—the Midianites did, after all, inflict severe damage on the Israelites before being driven

One of the earliest known representations of a horseman, Egyptian *circa* 1350 B.C. These riders were not armed and were used only as messengers. The first mounted warrior occurs in the Aramaean army in the 10th century B.C., though the Kadesh (1288) reliefs show such a messenger armed with a bow (for self defence?), and another from the tomb of Horemheb (second half of 14th century) shows the rider carrying a throwing stick. The painted white lines may represent a natural piebald hide, or may reflect the Egyptian practice of chalking such markings on the animals. (Author's collection)

Late Hittite chariot from Zinjirli. The Hittites used their chariots primarily for close combat, each carrying two warriors and a driver, the former armed with spears and shields as well as bows. Note that the axle is under the centre of the body (necessary because of the heavier load carried) which made the chariot less manoeuvrable and slower than the Egyptian examples, which were designed as mobile missile platforms only. (Arkeoloji Müzeleri Müdürlüğü, Istanbul)

out. Some tribesmen fought in the Palestinian and Syrian armies from time to time: thus at Qarqar (853) the Aramaeans were supported by 'Gindibu the Arab' who supplied 1,000 camels, and therefore we must suppose 1,000 riders and another 1,000 bowmen. The reliefs of Ashurbanipal's campaigns against rebellious Arab tribes in the mid-7th century reveal that even at this late date the Arabs were still fighting totally unarmoured, on foot or mounted on camels in pairs, and armed with only a simple bow.

The Aramaeans (Syrians)

Originally known as the Syrians, the Aramaeans were so named by the Israelites, from *Aram-naharaim*, meaning 'the land between two rivers' (i.e. the Tigris and Euphrates). By the 10th century the Aramaeans were a large, rich and well-established people whose technical knowledge was comparable to that of the Philistines. However, the Aramaeans were normally split into many petty and mutually hostile kingdoms, of which the most notable was Damascus.

Their army contained infantry and chariots, and was the first to include mounted warriors, possibly the earliest of all cavalry. The army's strength was formidable: the kingdoms of Zobah, Beth-Rehob, Maacah and Tob sent 40,000 men to fight the Israelites under David.

The main source of information on Aramaean armies of the following (9th) century is a document of Shalmaneser III, which lists the forces fielded by the Syro-Palestinian alliance which defeated the Assyrians at Qarqar in 853. The figures given are probably exaggerated to explain the Assyrian defeat, but they do serve to indicate the likely proportion of each arm and the comparative strengths of the various kingdoms; the allies are not included here. *Damascus*: 1,200 chariots, 1,200 cavalry, 20,000 infantry. *Siana* (Shian): 30 chariots, 10,000 infantry. *Arqad*: ten chariots, 10,000 infantry. *Musri*: 1,000 infantry. *Ammon*: 1,000 infantry. *Que*: 500 infantry. *Usanata* (Usnu): 200 infantry. Total: 1,240 chariots, 1,200 cavalry, 42,700 infantry. Some authorities translate 'cavalry' as outriggers (i.e. spare horses for the chariots), but the Aramaeans are known to have been using mounted soldiers in the preceding century and there is no reason to suppose that the 1,200 cavalry were anything but that.

Bearing in mind that each chariot had a crew of two, the Aramaeans must therefore have had 3,680 mounted men to 42,700 foot, approximately 11.5 per cent. The charioteers were armed with bows; the infantry were divided into shock troops armed with spears and shields and their supporting light troops with bows and slings. The mounted men of the 10th century were equipped with helmets and shields and armed with either a bow, javelin or spear.

The Israelites
The Israelites were Semites (apparently of Aramaean stock) who, in the 14th century B.C., migrated from Mesopotamia (along with other Semites who founded Ammon, Edom and Moab) and penetrated into south-east Palestine. By the following century they had conquered and settled that land, adopting the Canaanite language. By about 1000 B.C. they had occupied the land on both sides of the Jordan from the Dead Sea to approximately the northern limit of the Waters of Merom.

There were historically ten tribes of Israel (Simeon and Judah being excluded) which settled in Canaan: Asher, Zebulun, Dan, Naphtali, Issachar, Ephraim, Benjamin, Gad, Reuben, and Manasseh. A thirteenth tribe, that of Levi, was

not granted land in the Israelites' new country.

When Deborah defeated the Canaanites in the 12th century she is believed to have commanded an army of not less than 10,000 men, and possibly as many as 20,000. Thereafter the Israelite army grew in strength until in the reign of Saul (*c.*1040–1012), when the tribes were united to fight the Philistines, it numbered possibly 33,000 warriors. Saul was the first to form a 'royal bodyguard', a small regular standing army to provide the nucleus round which the tribal levies could muster. This guard numbered some 3,000 men divided into three 'companies', the normal division of formations in the Israelite army. Two of these companies served under Saul personally, the third under his eldest son Jonathan. There is no precise information on how the tribal levies were organized.

Hittite infantry at Kadesh, as portrayed at the Ramesseum, Thebes. The 'striped clothing' illustrated in these reliefs and referred to as such in popular English publications, is in fact the artists' stylization of scale armour. The charioteers wore scale armour, but the infantry seem to have been unarmoured. The heavy infantry would have had shields and possibly a head defence. (From Baikie)

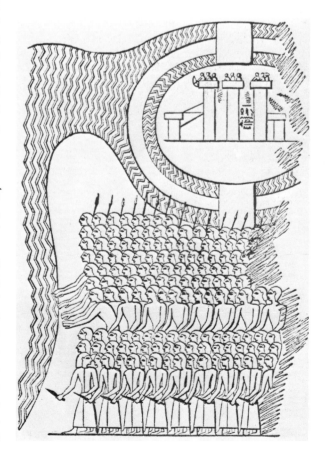

David (c.1012–972) defeated the Philistines, only to have civil war flare up between Judah and Israel. The two kingdoms were eventually united by David and thereafter the United Monarchy became a leading military power in Palestine and Syria.

Whilst in exile, David had formed a small band of warriors known as The Thirty, recruited from amongst the Trans-Jordanians. Later this band grew to 400 in number, and eventually 600. When he attained the crown of Judah, David recruited a second band, and these two bands formed the nucleus of his regular army, or royal guard. His top military commanders were all men who had served in the first band, and were still known as The Thirty, but were now an army council which was largely responsible for framing regulations, deciding appointments and promotions, and handling other military matters. The commanders of the tribal militias were also drawn from The Thirty.

The Israelites of the royal guard formed a 'corps' known as the *gibborim* or mighty men. A second regular 'corps' was recruited from outside the United Monarchy, mostly from the Philistines. David's original band had itself fought as mercenaries in the army of the Philistine Achisk, king of Gath, and when David became king he recruited many of his second corps from Gath (there were around 600 Gittites in all), as well as from the

Cherethites and Pelethites, men he had also met whilst in exile. This mercenary corps was used mainly to deal with internal clashes, and played a decisive part in the battle with David's son Absalom. The mercenary corps was commanded by Benaiah ben Jehoiada, with Ittai, a Gittite, as second-in-command. The entire standing army was commanded by Joab.

The standing army initially consisted entirely of infantry, but there are indications that as the Israelites crushed their enemies and moved down from the hills, so chariots and possibly some cavalry were introduced into the regular army. Thus in Chronicles (1) XVIII:3–4 we read that David, after defeating the Aramaean king Hadarezer and capturing 7,000 horsemen (or horses?) and 100 chariots, hamstrung the horses, 'but reserved of them 100 chariots'. It seems only logical that the Israelites should adopt the methods of warfare of their enemies as they moved on to the coastal plain; Aramaeans, Philistines and Canaanites all had chariots, while the Aramaeans had cavalry by the 10th century, i.e. towards the end of David's reign.

The bulk of the Israelite army was formed by the tribal levies, organized in a complex system whereby every able-bodied man over 20 served a compulsory national service. The entire militia force consisted of 12 corps each of 24,000 men, with one corps on active service for one month of the year, and the other 11 going about their everyday life, but as reservists. The unique factor about this organization was that for the first time David

Carts of the Sea Peoples, as depicted on the reliefs at Medinet-Habu. (From Wilkinson)

Chariot of the 1405–1370 period, believed to be a Canaanite one taken to Egypt (where it was found) as a gift or booty. Note the axle is at the extreme rear edge of the body to give maximum speed and manoeuvrability, and the body floor is of woven thongs. The long axle (1.53 metres) gave great stability on sharp turns. (Author's collection)

succeeded in breaking the purely tribal loyalties, since each corps contained contingents from all the tribes. However, this was not due to the emergence of nationalism, but rather because of a personal loyalty to David himself. The full list of officers responsible for maintaining the individual corps in the field may be found in the Bible: Chronicles (1) XXVII:1–21. Chronicles (1) XXI:5 lists the total number of warriors available to David as: 'And there were in Israel 800,000 valiant men that drew swords.' Twelve times 24,000 gives only 288,000, a more likely figure. Amasa ben Jeter was in overall command of this national militia.

The militia corps were organized in units of 1,000, sub-divided into units of 100, 50 and ten. A description of these sub-units and their officers may be found in Deuteronomy I:15.

In David's time this army consisted entirely of infantry, grouped according to weapon, which was itself determined by tribe, as each tribe used the traditional weapon or weapons best suited to its aptitude. This tribal specialization is listed to some extent in Chronicles (1) XII. Briefly it is as follows: Benjamin: archers and slingers, at least 700 of whom were ambidextrous. Gad, Reuben and half Manasseh: sword and buckler men, also archers. Zebulun: expert 'with all instruments of war, 50,000 which could keep rank', suggesting spearmen in phalanx formation. Naphtali: spear and shield. Dan and Asher: 'expert in war'. The men of Issachar seem to have specialized in raiding and scouting missions.

Finally there was a 'homeguard' of Levite settlements on the borders of the newly acquired lands in Canaan. The Levites had a religious zeal which made them especially reliable troops for unstable border areas.

Contrary to legend, David's successor, Solomon, was not a wise king; on his death, as a result of discontent fostered during his reign, the United Monarchy split and civil war erupted. Solomon's army is listed in Kings (1) IV:26 as: 'And Solomon had 40,000 stalls and horses for his chariots, and 1,200 horsemen.' In Kings (1) X:26: 'And Solomon gathered together chariots and horsemen: and he had 1,400 chariots, and 12,000 horsemen, whom he bestowed in the cities for chariots, and with the king at Jerusalem.' And in Chronicles (2) IX:25: 'And Solomon had 4,000 stables for horses and chariots, and 12,000 horsemen.' The most likely figures here are 4,000 stables for horses and chariots (i.e. 1,400 chariots, with two horses and one reserve each) and 1,200 horsemen.

By the late 9th century the power of Israel and Judah had declined: we read in Kings (2) XIII:7

of '50 horsemen, and ten chariots, and 10,000 infantry; for the king of Syria had destroyed them' as the total force available to these two kingdoms. Yet at Qarqar (853) Ahab had been able to furnish 2,000 chariots and 10,000 infantry to help Damascus against the Assyrians.

It seems likely that the Israelite chariots were grouped in 'divisions' of 150, for Ahab's stables at Megiddo had room for 450 horses. The 150 was probably divided into three sub-units: in 722, after the fall of Samaria, Sargon II formed a unit of 50 chariots from the remnants of the defeated Israelite army.

The Judaeans

The Judaeans also had a small regular army or royal guard and a national militia. The regular troops included mercenaries from Chereti and Pelethi, and in the 10th century charioteers and an élite infantry called 'runners', believed to be light infantry trained to operate with the small chariot force. Organization was also in units of ten, 50,

Enemies of the Egyptians of the New Kingdom. Top row: two Sherden and two Philistine warriors; three unidentified warriors, possibly Asiatics or Canaanites, some of whom are known to have worn helmets with long feathers stuck to the crown, their points meeting at the top; four Libyans identified by their side lock and genital sheath. Bottom row: man from Punt; three men referred to as *Shari*, probably a tribe from northern Arabia, and four Syrians (Rot-n-n) in typical long white robes with coloured 'piping'. The Syrians had a light complexion, blue eyes, and brown or reddish hair. (From Wilkinson)

100 and 1,000, with a total levy of around 100,000 men. The levy was divided into five corps which in the days of Jehoshaphat (c.876–851) were listed as: 30,000 commanded by Adnah, 28,000 under Jehohanan, 20,000 under Amasiah, 18,000 archers under Jehozabad, and 20,000 archers under Eliada of Benjamin. (In fact the Bible adds a nought to each of these totals, but that would give over one million warriors, an unacceptable figure.)

The kingdom was divided into 12 administrative divisions, but there were insufficient men in each division to serve as the active force on a monthly rota. Instead it is believed each of the five divisions either served for $10\frac{1}{2}$ weeks a year, or served at half strength for two terms of five weeks per year.

The warriors were almost all infantrymen, the phalanx of Judah being famous: presumably the 78,000 men of Adnah, Jehohanan and Amasiah were mostly spearmen.

The Assyrians

In the days of the Early Empire (1400–885) the Assyrian army was recruited almost entirely from the general population in times of crisis, and the only regular troops were a royal bodyguard of perhaps 1,000 men, which must have crewed most of the chariot force and also provided trained officers to command the levies.

Each provincial governor in Assyria or in the conquered territories probably had a similar but smaller bodyguard of regular troops, and was responsible for mustering the levies in his area as needed. The basic unit in these early armies appears to have been 1,000 men.

This levy system still applied at the beginning of the Late Empire (885–626), although Ashurnasirpal II made some changes towards a more permanent force, made the chariots heavier, and introduced the first cavalry units, recruited from allies.

The next king, Tiglath-pileser III, introduced radical changes, forming a permanent standing army around the nucleus of the royal guard. This was essential for his ambitious plans of conquest, but also made the monarchy all-powerful—no longer dependent on the governors and aristocracy as it had been under the old feudal levy system. Under Tiglath-pileser III and his successor,

Bronze eye-axe, *circa* 1900. The eye-axe appeared *circa* 2100 and is so called because the points of the blade were extended back to the haft to form sockets. Such a blade was difficult to produce and demanded advanced technology. The Canaanites brought this style of axe to Egypt *circa* 1900 but it did not gain wide acceptance there. In Syria and Palestine the eye-axe was developed further to create a piercing axe—see p. 35. (By courtesy of Israel Dept of Antiquities and Museums)

Sargon II, the new Assyrian state was built around this regular army, commanded by the king or his eldest son, the Rab-Shakeh (vizier), or by the Turtan (chief general). The army was divided into wings of approximately 15,000 men, each commanded by a royally appointed general, and subdivided into *Kisri* of between 50 and 200 men. In addition, all conquered peoples had to transfer the services of the bulk of their army to the Assyrian army.

The infantry always constituted the largest part of the Assyrian armies, a rough estimate of proportions of troop types being one chariot to ten

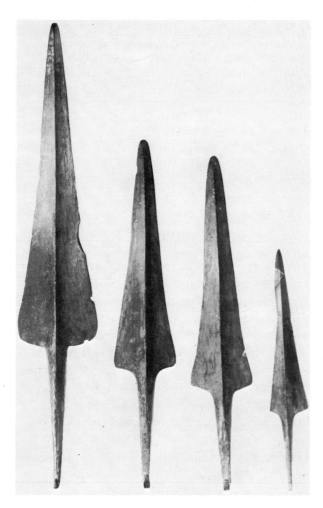

Bronze spear and javelin heads from the Megiddo area, *circa* 2100–1900. Note the ends of the tangs are turned back to help prevent splitting of the haft on impact. This problem was not solved until the introduction of socketed heads in the first half of the second millennium. (By courtesy of Israel Dept of Antiquities and Museums)

corps remained essentially Assyrian.

Tiglath-pileser III increased the strength of the chariot corps by adding a third crew member to each chariot, and the trend towards bigger and heavier chariots continued under Ashurbanipal, who added a fourth man to each crew. By his reign, therefore, the chariot corps had lost much of its speed and manoeuvrability, but, combined with the rapid growth of the cavalry arm, this reform meant that the Assyrian army now had a large proportion of its men mounted either on horseback or in chariots, and was thus able to strike suddenly by moving large numbers of men at greater speed than their enemies.

The strength of the Assyrian armies is rarely given in the contemporary records, which are more concerned with listing enemy dead and booty. At Qarqar in 853 Shalmaneser III had 120,000 men, and Sennacherib had 185,000 when he took Jerusalem in 699. If proportions of troop types were as mentioned above, then Shalmaneser may have had approximately 1,100 chariots and 11,000 cavalry, while Sennacherib may have had about 1,600 chariots and 16,000 cavalry: in both cases approximately nine per cent of the armies may have been mounted.

The constant rebellions of the 7th century gradually eroded the strength of Assyria by killing off large numbers of the sturdy Assyrian peasantry, and the later kings (Sennacherib, Esarhaddon and Ashurbanipal) were forced to rely more and more on mercenaries, mostly recruited from the wild Scythian tribes along the empire's northern frontier.

Apart from their ruthless policies of extermination and deportation, to smash forever a conquered people's identity, and their highly organized professional army, the Assyrians had one other vital ingredient for success—iron. As early as *circa* 1000 B.C. their militia was equipped with some weapons and armour of iron, but references to iron weapons and armour first become really numerous in the years 890–883, just before the emergence of Assyria as the leading power under Ashurnasirpal. By the time of Sargon II the Assyrians were so rich in iron that their army was completely equipped with iron weapons and armour, and a single room in Sargon's palace has yielded no less than 150 tons of unworked bars of iron during excavations.

cavalry to 100 infantry. The infantry was grouped in national and regional corps, each specializing in the weapons and tactics best suited to the men's temperament and their traditional methods of fighting. Thus the stolid Assyrian peasant, backbone of the army, was armed mostly with spear and shield to form the phalanx of shock-troops, whose slow but irresistible advance was the culminating phase in a typical Assyrian battle plan. The auxiliary corps of allies and conquered peoples were most often composed of light archers or light cavalrymen. Slingers were not introduced into the army until the reign of Sennacherib (705–681). Heavy archers, heavy cavalry and the chariot

The Plates

A1 *Sumerian heavy infantryman, circa 2500 B.C.*
First known example of the classical heavy infantryman, armed with all-covering shield and long spear, and fighting in a tight-packed phalanx. The phalanx, coupled with the ability to manufacture bronze weapons and the innovation of the war chariot, enabled the Sumerians to crush all opposition and create the first 'empire'. The figure is based on the Standard of Ur panel in the British Museum and the Stele of Vultures in the Louvre, both dated *circa* 2500 B.C. In the past the stylized representation of six warriors to a rank, signified by six roundels on the shields and six spears protruding between each pair of shields, has been misinterpreted, and the shield has been portrayed incorrectly with six discs instead of a single central boss. Interpretations of the kilt usually show a cloth with a 'dagged' edge, but some contemporary relief carvings seem to indicate a series of hanks of wool or hair side by side. The illustrator has chosen the interpretation of a series of long 'tassels', perhaps of goat hair. This would in fact give both ease of movement and some measure of protection in battle.

A2: *Egyptian heavy infantryman, 19th Dynasty*
Prior to this period the Egyptian infantryman had been unarmoured, wearing just a kilt and armed with a spear and shield. However, warfare first against the Hyksôs, and then against the Canaanites and Sea Peoples had led to the introduction of armour for heavy infantry. Basic defences were the shield, a 'cuirass' of padded linen, and a triangular front piece of stiffened linen on the kilt or *shenti*. Arms were the spear and either an axe or a *khopesh*, the mace having declined in importance with the arrival of armoured enemies.

A3: *Egyptian archer, 19th Dynasty*
Archers were the vital corps of the Egyptian army, whether on foot or in chariots. This light foot archer is unarmoured except for a quilted head-dress, but heavy archers and those in chariots had the padded 'cuirass'. We cannot be certain of clothing colours, but the Egyptians had a knowledge of mordant dyes, and used red, blue, green, yellow and brown in various shades in addition to white, black and grey. They did not have lilac, purple, orange, crimson or olive green. Clothing was predominantly white according to surviving paintings, but some was striped or patterned, generally with red or blue, and coloured borders made up of a number of thin lines were quite common.

Bronze 'duck-bill axe' of the 19th century B.C. The Syrian and Palestinian eye-axe was improved by lengthening the blade and narrowing its edge, thus developing a socketed axe capable of piercing metal helmets and body armour. The duck-bill axe remained in use until the 18th century, by which time the blade had been made even narrower, so that it resembled the chisel-like axe of the Sumerians. (By courtesy of Israel Dept of Antiquities and Museums)

Assyrian warriors of the time of Sargon II (721–705) from reliefs at his palace. The high-laced boot first appeared in Sargon II's reign, the quilted (?) trousers in the same period. The curved shield at right was introduced during the reign of Tiglath-Pileser III (745–727). (From Layard)

B: *Sumerian chariot bearing King Eannatum of Lagash, circa 2500 B.C.*

This illustration is based on information contained in the Standard of Ur panel and the Stele of Vultures. The artists who produced these great

Crest of helmet from Lachish, Israel, *circa* 1200–920, the Biblical period which covers the Judges and early Kings. (By courtesy of Israel Dept of Antiquities and Museums)

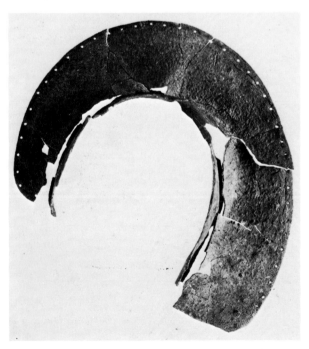

works of art did not understand perspective and showed the various faces of objects flat. Thus, in contemporary works of art, the Sumerian chariot is portrayed side view, but with the front added to the forward edge of the side, and as recently as the 1950s this has led to respected authors and journals publishing illustrations which are incorrect. Excavated evidence gives no indication of a swivelling front axle; and the fact that the onagers were restrained by a device as crude as a ring through the upper lip suggests that their level of training and co-ordination was not high. The chariot was therefore probably used at a fairly slow pace. Again, we interpret the kilt effect in the carvings as being of hair.

C: *Chariot of the Pharaoh Rameses II, 1288 B.C.*
Based on a magnificent 13th century relief in the Ramesseum at Thebes, this portrays the Egyptian chariot at the height of its evolution—extremely light, fast and manoeuvrable. Rameses II is shown wearing a full length coat of scale armour, a most unusual protection, but presumably essential if the Pharaoh was to risk his life in the confused chariot/archery skirmish which preceded the clash of the infantry. Egyptian chariots were designed to assault the enemy's main line from a distance with archery, and so weaken it for an infantry attack. Enemy chariots tried to prevent this happening and do the same to the Egyptian infantry and, as the chariot forces became ever bigger, so this preliminary skirmish for chariot supremacy tended to become the crisis of a battle. The contemporary painting on which this plate is

based shows the Pharaoh fighting the Hittite chariots at Kadesh, a battle won by the Egyptian chariots, for the Hittite infantry did not enter the battle at all.

Angus McBride writes: Interpretation of contemporary material which follows rigid artistic conventions of which we have only an imperfect understanding is always extremely difficult. The scale corselet worn by the Pharaoh is almost certainly bronze, since the Egyptians generally indicated bronze and electrum in blue, due to their limited palette; I believe the alternate bands of blue and yellow shown in the original painting are a convention adopted by the artist to indicate the laced construction. The war-crown was of blue leather with discs of either bronze or electrum rivetted or sewn all over it; the detail drawings show front and rear elevations.

I have interpreted the round decorations on the yoke as discs with engraved or relief motifs; some sources interpret these as spheres, but no other contemporary Egyptian artefact known to me suggests that the craftsmen of the period had mastered the necessary techniques. The addition of guide-rings to the yoke is my own interpretation based on study of the practical problems involved. The body of the chariot is shown in the sketch in side elevation; the solid areas were of blue leather with gold decoration. The two quivers sloping backwards contain arrows, their delicate fletchings protected from damage at each end by decorated rods. The forward-sloping case contains two bows, and the grip and hand-guard of an 'eye-axe' can also be seen.

D1: *Nubian archer, 19th Dynasty*
The Nubians were noted archers and large numbers fought for the Egyptians. Their chiefs wore ostrich and other feathers on their heads, and large circular earrings of gold, as well as gold collars and bracelets. This figure is based on Nubian archers illustrated in the reliefs at Beit el-Weli (1290–1223): similar paintings on the walls of Huy's tomb at Thebes show the Nubians with reddish-brown skin, the Kushites with black skin. It is probable that the Nubians, with their mixed Hamitic and Egyptian blood, though still possessing negroid features, were of a lighter skin colour than the purer negro stock of those Kushites living west of the Nile.

D2: *Philistine heavy infantryman, 20th Dynasty*
According to reliefs at Medinet Habu, on which this figure is based, there was only the one type of Philistine warrior: a heavy infantryman equipped with two spears as short-range missiles, and a sword for close combat. He is protected by a helmet with hair crest, a tunic with overlapping leather strips, and has the light buckler of the sword fighter.

The interpretation of the crest as hair rather

Crests and bridles of a riding horse (left) and chariot horses, from reliefs at the palace of Sargon II at Khorsabad. (From Layard)

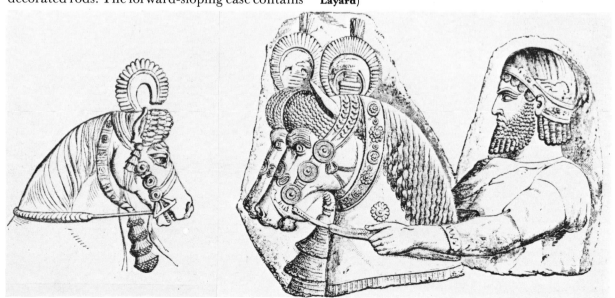

than feathers is based on study of Egyptian artistic convention; their representations of feathers were precise and unvarying, and the artist seems here to have been attempting to convey another material for which there was no set convention in his canon. The body-armour could be of leather strips, or of leather with some bronze reinforcement.

D3: *Sherden warrior, 19th Dynasty*
This figure is also based on the Medinet Habu reliefs and is equipped much as the Philistine, except the Sherden are not shown with spears. The distinctive helmet seems to have had only horns initially, the central disc (*not* 'ball' as it is usually described) not being added until after the Sea Peoples were defeated and therefore presumably connected with the Egyptian sun god Re. Our interpretation of the body-armour as linen or thin leather, presumably in padded layers, is based on the fact that Egyptian sources show the armour as being tied with thongs of the same material as the

Parthian shot: mounted archer fleeing from Assyrian cavalry, from a relief in Ashurnasirpal's palace at Nimrud. The high boots with turned up toes and conical cap (probably of felt), and the mode of fighting—described by ancient authors as being peculiar to the Parthian and Persian tribes —all suggest this is an early representation of one of those Median tribesmen who finally overwhelmed the Assyrian empire. (From Layard)

armour itself. They also seem to make a point of showing the bronze sword as longer than that of the Philistines.

E1: *Semite archer, 12th Dynasty*
This figure is taken from a wall painting in the tomb of Khnumhotep III at Beni-Hasan, which shows a caravan of Semites *en route* to Egypt, armed with the typical weapons of Canaan in the 2100–1570 period. The archer has a double-convex bow, quiver, and 'duck-bill' axe. Other warriors in the painting are either similarly armed or carry a spear and hurling stick. All are totally unarmoured.

E2: *Shasu-Bedouin warrior, 19th Dynasty*
Based on reliefs in the rock temple at Beit el-Weli in Nubia, which show the Pharaoh Rameses II defeating the Libyan-Nubian alliance. All the Shasu illustrated in the reliefs wear the same type of clothing, but at least two types of turban are shown, presumably denoting tribe. All are armed with one or two short spears (javelins?) and some carry a *khopesh*, as shown here.

E3: *Libyan archer, 20th Dynasty*
Taken from the same source as the Shasu tribesman, this warrior's nationality can be recognised instantly by the distinctive side-lock of hair and the genital sheath, both unique to the Libyans. A 20th Dynasty relief at Medinet Habu shows captive Libyans wearing a full length cloak, whilst the Beit el-Weli reliefs show captives clad only in a loincloth. The cloak probably provided some degree of protection in battle, as well as being an essential item of clothing on campaign.

F1: *Syrian archer, 18th Dynasty*
The clothing of this warrior is based on wall paintings from the tomb of Rekhmire (vizier to Thutmose III) at Thebes and illustrates the distinctive clothing of the Syrians. He is armed with a triangular (composite) bow, but has no other weapon.

F2: *Hittite charioteer, 13th century B.C.*
This warrior is based on information drawn from the Ramesseum at Thebes. The shield is of a distinctive shape and was probably either wickerwork or a wooden frame with hide covering. The

short boots with pointed toes are typically Hittite.

F3: *Hittite warrior of the Royal Guard, 9th century B.C.*
Based on the famous King's Gate relief at Car-chemish. Egyptian monuments of the earlier empire period all show the Hittites wearing long clothing with short sleeves, but the later monuments from the petty kingdoms show a short tunic ending just above the knees, and sometimes only a kilt of this length.

G1: *Assyrian infantryman, 7th century B.C.*
A spearman from the time of Ashurbanipal, based on a relief in the south-west palace at Nineveh. The infantryman of this period had much lighter equipment than his predecessors, relying mainly on the large shield and a helmet for defence. Some infantrymen, dressed and armed in the same style, carried wickerwork shields without hide or metal reinforcement.

G2: *Assyrian archer, 8th century B.C.*
Taken from an 8th century Assyrian relief, this light archer is protected by a belt, cross-straps and head-dress of padded linen, and is wearing a kilt with characteristic Assyrian pattern and fringe. However, he may be a Judaean serving in the Assyrian army, as the head-dress is typically Judaean. Other archers of the period are illustrated without the cross-straps or head-dress. All

Assyrian archers and cavalry of Ashurnasirpal's reign (885–859) from reliefs in his palace at Nimrud. (From Layard)

are armed with a composite bow and an iron sword.

G3: *Elamite archer, 7th century B.C.*
This figure is based on an Ashurbanipal relief at Nineveh, and can be distinguished from Assyrian light archers by the distinctive head-band and pattern on the quiver. He is armed with a compo-

Assyrian chariot from a bas-relief at Nimrud. The third crew member, to shield the other two, was added in the reign of Tiglath-Pileser III. The elliptical panel above the horses' backs was probably a strengthening rod covered by decorative material. It may also have served to divide the reins. (From Layard)

site bow and a long dagger or short sword of bronze.

H: *Assyrian mounted archer and Arab camel archer, 7th century B.C.*
Based on a relief from Ashurbanipal's palace at Nineveh, portraying that king's wars against the Arabs. The Arabs, unarmoured and equipped with only the simple bow, were easily crushed by the heavily armoured Assyrians with their iron weapons and composite bows. Arab infantry were similarly dressed and equipped, and are shown in the reliefs being overwhelmed by Assyrian heavy infantry and auxiliary archers.

Notes sur les planches en couleur

A1 Le premier exemple rencontré au cours de l'histoire du 'fantassin lourd', avec un grand bouclier, épieu long, et une tactique de combat en phalanx. **A2** Avant cette époque, le soldat égyptien combattait presque nu, mais les guerres contre le peuple Hyksôs (Pasteur), les chananéens et le 'peuple de la mer' amenèrent l'introduction d'une armure de lin raidi. **A3** Cet archer se bat à pied, et n'est protégé que par une coiffure de tissu molletonné; ceux qui se battaient en chariot, et les archers d'infanterie lourde étaient également revêtus d'une cuirasse molletonnée.

B Cette illustration est tirée du panneau 'L'Etendard d'Ur' et de la Stele des Vautours, maintenant au Louvre. Les reconstructions précédentes étaient erronées, à cause d'une erreur d'interprétation des conventions particulières de perspective, de rigueur dans l'art sumérien.

C Tiré du panneau en relief du Ramesseum à Thèbes—XIIIème siècle avant Jésus Christ. On peut voir le pharaon combattant contre les hittites à Kadesh. Son manteau à armure en écailles est peu commun, et est peut-être propre au monarque.

D1 Un grand nombre de ces archers de Nubie se battirent pour l'Egypte. Leurs chefs avaient des plumes sur la tête, et de larges boucles d'oreilles, colliers et bracelets d'or. **D2** Typique de la plupart des guerriers phillistins, cette figure est copiée des reliefs de Médinet-Abou. Ce guerrier porte deux épieux, une épée et un bouclier léger. Il est protégé grâce à un casque à crête crinée et une tunique bardée. **D3** Il est possible qu'à l'origine le casque ne portait que des cornes, et que le disque central ait été ajouté ultérieurement—peut-être en référence au dieu soleil Râ.

E1 Une peinture murale à Béni-Hasan montre des guerriers chananéens, les uns armés de l'arc convexe double et d'une hache à bec recourbé, et les autres d'un épieu et d'une lance-javeline. Ils n'ont aucune armure. **E2** Sculptures du temple de Béit el-Wéli en Nubie, montrant des guerriers, les uns armés seulement d'une ou deux javelines, et d'autres avec également un kopesh. **E3** On peut reconnaître les guerriers libyens au style distinctif de leur coiffure et de leur protection génitale sur les sculptures de Beit el-Wéli. Une sculpture à Médinet-Abou nous montre un long manteau—peut-être était-il porté pour se protéger pendant le combat, et aussi pour s'abriter en campagne?

F1 Ceci provient des peintures murales dans la tombe de Rekhmire à Thèbes, et montre le costume caractéristique syrien. L'arc est la seule arme visible. **F2** Le bouclier et les bottes courtes sont tous les deux particuliers aux hittites; cette figure est inspirée de murales visibles au Ramesseum, à Thèbes. **F3** Basé sur les célèbres sculptures de la Porte du Roi à Carchémis. Les sculptures plus anciennes représentent des vêtements longs à manches courtes, mais celles de provenance plus récente nous montrent des tuniques courtes, ou simplement des jupes courtes.

G1 Homme armé d'une lance de l'époque d'Assurbanipal, à partir d'une sculpture de Ninive. L'équipement est beaucoup plus léger qu'avant, et les guerriers sont protégés principalement par le bonclier et le casque. **G2** La jupe caractérisée par des frange et des dessins assyrien est portée, en association avec le couvre-chef rembourré, typiquement de Judée. Il est possible que la sculpture sur laquelle nous avons basé ce soldat représente un soldat de Judée, au service de l'Assyrie. **G3** Cette figure est basée sur les sculptures de Ninive; le couvre-chef caractéristique et le type de vêtements le distingue d'un archer léger assyrien.

H A partir d'une sculpture de Ninive, décrivant les guerres d'Assurbanipal contre les arabes. Ceux-ci furent facilement vaincus par les assyriens, mieux armés et mieux équipés.

Farbtafeln

A1 Das erste geschichtlich bekannte Beispiel des klassischen 'schweren Infanteriemannes', mit grossem Schild, langem Speer und Kampftaktiken in einer phalanx. **A2** Bevor dieser Periode kämpfte der egyptische Soldat fast nackt, jedoch Kriege gegen die Hyksôs, die Kanaaniten und die 'Seevölker' führten zu den Anfängen von Körperrüstung aus versteiftem Leinen. **A3** Dieser Bogenschütze kämpfte zu Fuss und ist nur geschützt durch eine wattierte Kopfbedeckung aus Stoff; diejenigen, die in Streit-wagen kämpften und Bogenschützen der schweren Infanterie, trugen auch eine wattierte Kürass.

B Diese Illustration ist basiert auf der Tafel 'Standard of Ur' und die 'Stele der Geier', jetzt im Louvre. Frühere Versuche der Wiedergabe waren dadurch ungenau, da die eigenartigen Vorstellungen der Perspektive, benutzt in der sumerischen Kunst, falsch verstanden wurden.

C Basiert auf der Relieftafel im Ramesseum bei Thebes—13. Jahrhundert v.Chr. Der Pharao ist gegen die Hittites bei Kadesh kämpfend gezeigt. Sein Mantel aus Schuppenpanzer ist ungewöhnlich und mag eine Eigenheit dieses Herrschers gewesen sein.

D1 Eine grosse Anzahl dieser nubianischen Bogenschützen kämpfte für Egypten. Ihre Führer waren ähnlich gekleidet, jedoch mit Federn auf dem Kopf und grossen goldenen Ohrringen, Kragen und Armbändern. **D2** Typisch für die meisten philistinischen Krieger, ist diese Figur einem Relief bei Medinet Habu entnommen. Er trägt zwei Speere und ein Schwert, sowie ein leichtes Schild und ist durch einen Helm mit Haarkrone und einer gepanzerten Tunika geschützt. **D3** Man glaubt, dass der Helm ursprünglich nur Hörner trug und dass die Mittelscheibe später zugefügt wurde—vielleicht in Bezugnahme auf den Sonnengott Re.

E1 Ein Wandgemälde bei Beni-Hasan zeigt einige Kanaaniten, bewaffnet mit dem Doppel-Konvex-Bogen und einer 'Entenschnabel'-Axt, und andere mit einem Speer und Wurfstock. Keiner trug irgendeine Art von Rüstung. **E2** Schnitzereien im Tempel bei Beit el-Weli in Nubien zeigen diese Krieger, manche davon nur mit ein oder zwei Wurfspiessen bewaffnet, andere mit einem kopesch hinzugefügt. **E3** Der besondere Stil der Frisur und die Geschlechtsscheide identifizieren die Libianer in den Beit el-Weli Schnitzereien. Eine Schnitzerei bei Medinet Habu zeigt, dass ein langer Umhang getragen wurde—vielleicht hatte es sowohl einen schützenden Wert in der Schlacht als auch für Unterschlupf sorgend im Feldzug.

F1 Dies ist von Wandmalereien im Grabmal von Rekhmire bei Thebes entnommen und zeigt das besondere syrische Kostüm. Der Bogen ist die einzige gezeigte Waffe. **F2** Beides, der Schild und die kurzen Stiefel sind besonders Hittite; diese Figur ist auf Material, zu sehen im Ramesseum bei Thebes, basiert. **F3** Basiert auf den berühmten Konigstor-Schnitzereien bei Carchemish. Frühere Schnitzereien zeigen lange Gewänder mit kurzen Ärmeln, jedoch spätere zeigen eine kurze Tunika, oder nur einen kurzen Rock.

G1 Speerwerfer von der Zeit von Ashurbanipal, basiert auf Schnitzereien bei Nineveh. Die Ausrüstung ist viel leichter als in früheren Perioden und der Schutz kommt hauptsächlich vom Schild und Helm. **G2** Der Rock aus charakteristischem assyrischem Muster und Fransenbesatz ist zusammen mit einer wattierten Kopfbedeckung, typisch judäisch, getragen; es ist möglich, dass diese Schnitzerei, auf der wir diesen Soldaten basieren, einen Judäer in assyrischem Dienst zeigt. **G3** Diese Figur ist auf Schnitzereien bei Nineveh basiert; das besondere Kopfband und das Muster am Köcher unterscheiden ihn von einem assyrischen leichten Bogenschützen.

H Von einer Schnitzerei im Palast des Ashurbanipal bei Nineveh, die Kriege des Königs gegen die Araber zeigend, die von den schwer bewaffneten und ausgerüsteten Assyrern leicht überwältigt wurden.